Control of Standard Business Terms: A Comparison Between the Systematic Approach of §§ 305 ff. BGB and Art. 496-498 of the Chinese Civil Code

Europäische Hochschulschriften Recht

European University Studies in Law

Publications Universitaires Européennes de Droit

Band/Volume 6729

Shuai Huang

Control of Standard Business Terms: A Comparison Between the Systematic Approach of §§ 305 ff. BGB and Art. 496-498 of the Chinese Civil Code

PETER LANG

Bibliografische Information der Deutschen Nationalbibliothek
Die Deutsche Nationalbibliothek verzeichnet diese Publikation in der Deutschen Nationalbibliografie; detaillierte bibliografische Daten sind im Internet über http://dnb.d-nb.de abrufbar.

Zugl.: Hamburg, Univ., Diss., 2022

D 18
ISSN 0531-7312
ISBN 978-3-631-89754-6 (Print)
E-ISBN 978-3-631-89883-3 (E-PDF)
E-ISBN 978-3-631-89884-0 (EPUB)
DOI 10.3726/b20740

Peter Lang – Berlin · Bern · Bruxelles · New York · Oxford · Warszawa · Wien

Diese Publikation wurde begutachtet.

www.peterlang.com

Die Fakultät Rechtswissenschaft der Universität Hamburg
hat diese Arbeit im Jahre 2022 als Dissertation angenommen.
Erstgutachter: Prof. Dr. Hinrich Julius
Zweitgutachter: Prof. Dr. Matthias Armgardt
Das Datum der mündlichen Prüfung: 27.10.2022

About the Author

Shuai Huang is a doctoral candidate of law under the supervision of Prof. Hinrich Julius at University of Hamburg with a scholarship from the China Scholarship Council. He passed the oral defense of his doctoral dissertation with the grade "magna cum laude" on October 27, 2022. The main field of his doctoral study is private law and comparative law. The other fields of his research include European and international law, law and economics, and national development. Shuai Huang got a master's degree in Chinese civil and commercial law from China's University of Political Science and Law. He got another master's degree in European and international law from University of Hamburg. He passed the National Judicial Examination of China in 2013.

Preface

This book is a doctoral dissertation accepted by the Faculty of Law of the University of Hamburg with the overall grade "magna cum laude" and funded by the China Scholarship Council.

I would like to express my sincere appreciation to Prof. Dr. Hinrich Julius for his supervision of this dissertation, and for his help during my four years in Germany. I would also like to express my sincere appreciation to Prof. Dr. Matthias Armgardt for the second expert opinion, and to Prof. Dr. Mareike Schmidt for her valuable questions in my oral defense. Special thanks should also go to Prof. Dr. Fei Yu, Dr. Jiangang Xu for their insightful suggestions as to my research.

This book is for Heidel, who is painting the blue sky in my sunshine. I would like to extend my deep gratitude to my family and friends, who supported me and shared with me my worries and happiness during my doctoral study, especially during the COVID-19 pandemic.

Contents

Introduction

1 Background

In May 2020, the Chinese Civil Code (hereafter abbreviated as CCC where necessary) was passed by the National People's Congress of China.[1] It is the first civil code in the history of the People's Republic of China. The CCC came into effect in January 2021. The contract part of the Chinese Civil Code comes from the Chinese Contract Law and is also profoundly influenced by the United Nations Convention on Contracts for the International Sale of Goods (CISG). However, unlike the other content within the contract part, the German Civil Code (Das Deutsche Bürgerliche Gesetzbuch, hereafter abbreviated as BGB where necessary) has rather influenced the regulations on control of standard business terms in the Chinese Civil Code. Evidence is that the Chinese Civil Code also has adopted the dichotomy of incorporation control and content control found in the German Civil Code. This influence is so substantial in the relevant Chinese academic studies that §§ 305 ff. BGB are an essential source of reference for Chinese literature in the discussion on those relevant Chinese regulations.

The control of standard business terms in the Chinese Civil Code is stipulated in Art. 496 and 497 CCC. Their predecessors, Art. 39 and Art. 40 of the Chinese Contract Law (hereafter abbreviated as CCL where necessary) took the Law Regulating the Standard Business Terms (Gesetz zur Regelung des Rechts der Allgemeinen Geschäftsbedingungen, hereafter abbreviated as AGBG where necessary) as an important object of reference in its drafting,[2] but continuous revisions and simplifications in the process of drafting made it that Art. 39 and 40 CCL became considerably different from the regulations of the AGBG. Art. 39 and 40 CCL encountered problems later in practice. These problems included the unclear legal consequence of incorporation control in Art. 39 CCL and the vague criteria of content control in Art. 40 CCL.

Such challenges have prompted Chinese legal scholars to constantly call for amendments during the CCC's legislative process.[3] As a result, in the

1 See State Council of People's Republic of China, Civil Code of the People's Republic of China, available at http://english.www.gov.cn/archive/lawsregulations/202012/31/content_WS5fedad98c6d0f72576943005.html

2 See HE Xuxu, FXJ 2018, no. 6, p. 175.

3 See LIU Chengwei, FXZZ 2019, no. 3, p. 35; HAN Shiyuan, FXZZ 2019, no. 3, p. 27; ZHANG Liang, SSDX 2019, no. 1, p. 135.

amendments adopted by the legislator of the CCC, the role of incorporation control under Art. 496 II CCC is clarified further: Art. 496 II CCC concerns incorporation control and prescribes the same legal consequence as § 305 II BGB. Consequently, the Chinese Civil Code and the German Civil Code became more similar on the issue of control of standard business terms. This illustrates the influence of the German Civil Code on the legislation of the Chinese Civil Code.

Although the Chinese legislator also made revisions to Art. 497 CCC, Art. 40 CCL and Art. 497 CCC still share the common legislative mode, the core conceptions of which are the "liability" and the "main right." This legislative mode does not detail how to find the concrete content of the liability or the main right.[4] The criteria of content control remain unclear because of this legislative mode. This legislative mode is very different from that in the German Civil Code. The German influence and the difference on the legislative mode raise the question of whether Art. 497 CCC could be interpreted based on the German Civil Code in order to clarify the criteria of content control in the Chinese Civil Code.

In addition to the interpretation of Art. 497 CCC, the bigger picture is how one can differentiate between B2B and B2C contracts in the control of standard business terms. This is the common problem shared by both the German Civil Code and Chinese Civil Code. As mentioned above, there are, to some degree, approaches to this differentiation in Chinese legal practice. However, these approaches are far from definite or stable, raising no fewer questions than those in German law. More importantly, these approaches have never been systematically discussed and summarized in Chinese literature. On the contrary, in Germany there are many discussions on this issue, but like for the Chinese case, still no commonly accepted answer. From this angle, China and Germany stand in a similar situation, and both require a solution to differentiate between B2B and B2C contracts in control of standard business terms in a reasonable way.

2 The Comparative Legal Study and the Questions to Answer

Despite the influence of the German Civil Code, Art. 496-498 CCC are not the same as §§ 305 ff. BGB. Compared with §§ 305 ff. BGB, there are indeed some equivalent rules in Art. 496-498 CCC, while some are similar, and others are simply different. What is more, there are also similarities and differences between the relevant German and Chinese judicial practices on control of standard

4 See Chapter 3, part 2 of this dissertation.

business terms. The comparison between Chinese law and German law should also involve these judicial practices.

One specific issue in the above comparison is the differences between B2B standard business terms and B2C standard business terms. This issue is one of the most important problems faced by both Chinese law and German law. There are, to some degree, differentiated paths to control B2C and B2B standard business in the Chinese legal practice despite the fact that there is nearly no legislative differentiation between their control in the Chinese Civil Code.[5] This is the opposite situation to German law. In Germany, the legislative differentiation between the B2C and B2B standard business terms remains blurred by the German legal practice.[6]

This solution could be a legislative solution or a solution of legal interpretation but it must be first be theoretically established. In other words, the justification of the differentiated control between B2B and B2C contracts should first be discussed. The starting point of this discussion could be a classification of B2B transactions into groups in need of different strictness of standard business terms control.[7] This will also be one of the emphases of this dissertation.

Another issue is how to clarify the unclear criteria of content control in Art. 497 CCC by borrowing German criteria of content control. Because of the influence of German law to the Chinese regulations on this issue, it is meaningful to explore a new interpretation of Art. 497 CCC with reference to the German relevant regulations and judicial practice on content control. This issue involves both the understandings of German law and Chinese law on the content control rules.

With the consideration of the influence of German law to Chinese law on control of standard business terms, an understanding of §§ 305 ff. BGB is able to provide important insights into the interpretation of Art. 497 CCC. A comparison between the German Civil Code and the Chinese Civil Code can also help to solve the common problem faced by both of them, namely the differentiation between B2B and B2C contracts.

This dissertation will firstly undertake a comprehensive comparison of §§ 305 ff. BGB and Art. 496-498 CCC. On the basis of this comparison, two core issues will be further discussed the two core issues, namely, the differentiation between B2B and B2C standard business terms and the interpretation of Art. 497

5 See Chapter 1, part 2.3.2, part 3.2.3 and part 4.2.1 of this dissertation.
6 See Chapter 2, part 3 of this dissertation.
7 See Chapter 4, part 3.1 of this dissertation.

CCC, the central regulation on content control of standard business terms in Chinese law.

This dissertation plans to answer the following questions:

(1) Which rules are the same, similar and different between the Chinese Civil Code and the German Civil Code concerning the control of standard business terms in terms of the legislation and legal practices?
(2) How can we deal with the common problem faced by both Germany and China that the control of standard business terms is not sufficiently differentiated between B2C and B2B standard business terms?
(3) Drawing on German legal experience, is it possible to solve the difficulties that are faced by the Chinese content control rules, which are to some extent similar to the approach of the German Civil Code?

This dissertation is divided into five chapters. Chapter 1 makes a comparison between the German Civil Code and the Chinese Civil Code on the issue of the control of standard business terms. On the basis of this comparison, this dissertation lists the particular challenges surrounding this issue in China and in Germany. Chapter 2 analyzes the problem shared by Germany and China: the differentiation between B2C contracts and B2B contracts. Chapter 3 analyzes the unique problem of the Chinese Civil Code, the unclear criteria for content control in Art. 497 CCC, and the relevant German legal experience. Next, in Chapters 4 and 5, the author attempts to find solutions to the previously analyzed problems. In Chapter 4, the author presents a theoretical frame through which to differentiate between the control of B2C and B2B standard business terms. This frame consists of a classification of B2C, B2C-like, and B2B transactions applicable both to Chinese law and German law on this issue. Finally, Chapter 5 attempts to interpret Art. 497 CCC based on the understanding of § 307 II BGB.

3 The Relevant Terminologies and Translations of Regulations

The terminology "standard business terms" is one of the several translations of Allgemeine Geschäftsbedingungen in the German Civil Code. Another translation is "general terms and conditions" or "terms and conditions." However, the terminology "general terms and conditions" or "terms and conditions" is not familiar in Chinese law, because Allgemeine Geschäftsbedingungen are usually mentioned as standard terms or formal standard contracts (格式条款 or 格式合同) in Chinese law. Thus, the terminology "standard business terms" used by this dissertation is a translation of compromise that both readers understand with a background of German or Chinese law.

This dissertation will repeatedly mention both sides of a contract containing standard business terms. The German Civil Code calls the party to the contract pre-formulating the standard business terms "the user" (Verwender). Although the Chinese Civil Code does not have a terminology as counterpart, "the user" is also understandable to Chinese lawyers. The other party to the contract to the contract is usually called "the contractual partner" (Vertragspartner) or "the other party to the contract" (Vertragsgegner), both of which are also understandable to Chinese lawyers. It is usually called "the other side" (对方) in Chinese Civil Code. In this dissertation, the author uses "the user" and "the contractual partner" to refer to each side of the contract respectively.

The author mostly translates the German Civil Code and the Chinese Civil Code by itself with the reference of the original versions in German and in Chinese. The official English translations of the German Civil Code[8] and of the Chinese Civil Code[9] are not used because there are a lot of the same terminologies translated into different English words in the German and Chinese official translations leading to inaccuracies.

8 The official translation of the German Civil Code of the Federal Office of Justice, available at https://www.gesetze-im-internet.de/englisch_bgb/.

9 The official translation of the Chinese Civil Code of the National People's Congress, available at http://www.npc.gov.cn/englishnpc/c23934/202012/f627aa3a4651475db936899d69419d1e/files/47c16489e186437eab3244495cb47d66.pdf.

Chapter 1: A Comparison Between German Law and Chinese Law on Control of Standard Business Terms

The comparison of German law and Chinese law on the control of standard business terms in this dissertation, constitutes the basis for the analysis and solution of the selected problems. The focus of this comparison is the similar regulations between the German law and the Chinese law. This comparison aims to summarize the German legal experience on the control of standard business terms. The German legal experience is how the German regulations control standard business terms. As the control of standard business terms of German law has a much longer history than that of Chinese law, how the German regulations control standard business terms is also precious knowledge to Chinese law. For this reason, how the German regulations control standard business terms is "experience" for Chinese law and we can call it "German legal experience." The German legal experience can be useful for the interpretation of the Chinese regulations if we can find in this chapter that the regulations of both countries are to deal with the similar or same issues and that there is ambiguity in the Chinese legal application. What is more, the common problem faced by the German regulations and the Chinese regulations on the control of standard business terms, namely, the differentiation between B2C and B2B standard business terms is only possible to be discussed after we find the present positions of the both countries' regulations in the legal comparison of this chapter.

1 The General Logic Behind Control of Standard Business Terms

The aim of the regulations on the control of standard business terms both in Chinese law and in German law is to protect the contractual partner faced with the standard business terms which have been unilaterally drafted by the user.[10] The conclusion of the contract containing standard business terms is mostly dominated by the user, where the contractual partner usually only has the chance to enjoy the formal freedom of contract, whereby they may decide to conclude

10 Cf. Lieb, AcP 178 (1978), 196 (200); Lindacher, BB 1972, 296 (297); WANG Liming, FSYJ 1994, no. 3, p. 73 f.; HAN Shiyuan, CCLR 1994 vol. 2 p. 455.

or not conclude a contract. However, they are not able to enjoy the material freedom of contract- namely, to take part in shaping the content of the contract.[11] The definition of standard business term is based on this process of contractual conclusion, the core of which is the lack of material freedom of contract. The definition of standard business term should clarify this core idea.[12]

The purpose of this protection of the contractual partner is to make sure that the content of standard business terms is not unreasonably disadvantageous to the contractual partner even without him or her participating in shaping the contract. The minimum requirement of this protection is that the contractual partner has the chance to understand the standard business terms used against them (incorporation control).[13] If the contractual partner does not have the chance to understand the standard business terms used against them, the courts do not need to check their concrete content, and these standard business terms should not be considered part of the contract. If the contractual partner has had this chance, the standard business terms are then subject a higher requirement: content control. In content control, the courts are required to check the reasonableness of the content of standard business terms materially.

Although the above general logic of the control of standard business terms is almost the same both for Chinese law and for German law, there are many differences in the concrete preconditions of the definition, incorporation control, and in content control of standard business terms between Chinese law and German law. The following will compare the similarities and differences in detail between the Chinese regulations and the German regulations of standard business terms.

2 The Definition of Standard Business Term: § 305 I BGB and Art. 496 I CCC

The definitions of standard business terms in the German Civil Code and the Chinese Civil Code are worded in almost the same way. The relevant practices in both countries to differentiate between standard business terms and individually negotiated terms are also similar. The most important difference between China and Germany is the differentiation between B2C and B2B standard business terms in judicial practices.

---

11 Cf. Heinrich, S. 53; Höfling, S. 21 ff.

12 See Chapter 1, part 2 of this dissertation.

13 See Chapter 1, part 3 of this dissertation.

The two regulations, § 305 I BGB and Art. 496 I CCC state the following:

§ 305 I BGB:
"Standard business terms are all contract terms pre-formulated for more than two contracts (multiple-use) which one party to the contract (the user) presents to the other party (the contractual partner) upon the entering into of the contract. It is irrelevant whether the provisions take the form of a physically separate part of a contract or are made part of the contractual document itself, what their volume is, what typeface or font is used for them and what form the contract takes. Contract terms do not become standard business terms to the extent that they have been negotiated in detail between the parties."
Art. 496 I CCC
"A standard business term is a contractual term pre-formulated in advance by a party (the user) for the purpose of reuse which has not been negotiated with the other party (the contractual partner) when concluding the contract."

2.1 Multiple-Use or Reuse

2.1.1 Multiple-Use Criterion in § 305 I BGB

In Germany, the multiple-use of contractual terms is an element to constitute a standard business term according to § 305 I 1 BGB. Multiple-use means that standard business terms should be those contractual terms that are not drafted specifically for a single contract but serve as the basis for other contracts too.[14] But exceptionally, a B2C contractual term with no intention of multiple-use can also qualify as a standard business term (§ 310 BGB).

The judicial determination of multiple-use should be based on the user's intention rather than the fact that those contractual terms have been used multiple times. The wording of § 305 I 1 BGB does not require the intention to use those contractual terms with different contracting partners, and their use with one contracting partner is sufficient to qualify them as standard business terms.[15] In practice, however, the determination of multiple-use is usually based on the presumption built on the appearance of contractual terms,[16] which will be shortly discussed later.[17]

14 Staudinger/Mäsch § 305, Rn. 30; Erman/Roloff/Looschelders § 305 BGB, Rn. 11; BeckOGK/Becker § 305, Rn. 25.
15 BGH NJW 2004, 1454 (1455); BAG NZA 2006, 746 Rn. 20.
16 Cf. BGH NJW 2015, 1952 Rn. 30; BGHZ 157 102 (106 f.) = NJW 2004, 502 (503); BGH NJW-RR 2004, 814 (815); OLG Hamm NJW 2013, 392; OLG Düsseldorf NJW-RR 1997, 1147.
17 See Chapter 1, part 2.1.1.2 of this dissertation.

This is because the intention is decisive according to the wording of § 305 I BGB rather than the actual multiple-use.[18] This is because the intention is decisive according to the wording of § 305 I BGB rather than the actual multiple-use.[19]

To be qualified as standard business terms, contractual terms should be designed for a number of contracts, and under this premise, they are already standard business terms from the first use.[20] That means it is crucial whether the user of the contractual terms intended to use them for a number of contracts at the time when the first contract was concluded.[21] To determine this intention, the courts make a judicial determination based on the circumstances of the conclusion of the contract.[22] Pertinently, contractual terms are regularly considered to have been pre-formulated for multiple-use if they are intended to be used at least three times.[23]

Under the requirements of § 310 III Nr. 2 BGB, the requirement of multiple-use is not applicable to B2C contracts. Therefore, it is possible for contractual terms in single-use agreements to qualify as standard business terms while B2B contracts remain subject to the requirement of multiple-use.[24]

The intention of multiple-use is the first precondition for contractual terms to be qualified as standard business terms according to the wording of § 305 I 1 BGB.

2.1.1.1 The Appearance and Presumption of Multiple-Use

The above-mentioned multiple-use criterion is only based on the wording of § 305 I 1 BGB. Based on the appearance of contracts, specifically the content and design of the contractual terms, it is possible to judge whether the contractual terms are pre-formulated for multiple-use.[25] Those contractual terms which manifest themselves in a standard form show that the user intends for their multiple-use, unless proven otherwise.[26] Even if the user does not intend to use

---

18 Cf. BGH NJW 1999 2180 (2181); NJW 2988 (2989); NJW 2002, 138 (139) NJW 2004, 1454 (1455).

19 MüKoBGB/Basedow BGB § 305, Rn. 18.

20 BGH NJW 1981, 2343 (2344).

21 BGHZ 144, 242, NJW 2000, 2988; BGH WM 2008, 28.

22 BGH NJW 2000, 2988 (2989); NJW-RR 2002, 13 (14).

23 Cf. BGH NJW 2002, 138; 2004, 1454.

24 Cf. BGH WM 1991, 2069 (2070); NJW-RR 1988, 57 (58); MüKoBGB/Basedow BGB § 305, Rn. 17.

25 BGH NJW 2015, 1952 Rn. 30; BGHZ 157, 102 (106 f.) = NJW 2004, 502 (503); BGH NJW-RR 2004, 814 (815).

26 Graf v. Westphalen, NJW 2004, 1993 (1993); MüKoBGB/Basedow BGB § 305, Rn. 18.

the contractual terms more than three times, the contractual terms should considered standard business terms if they are a sample contract pre-formulated by a third party.[27] If the same contractual terms are actually used as a basis for several transactions, there is a presumption that they have been pre-formulated for this many transactions and accordingly, are to be regarded as standard business terms.[28]

The appearance of contracts simplifies the determination of the intention of multiple-use and thus makes it easier for contractual terms to qualify as standard business terms.

2.1.2 Reuse in Art. 496 I CCC

The precondition of "reuse" in Art. 476 I CCC is similar to the precondition of "multiple-use" in § 305 I BGB of the German Civil Code. According to the wording of Art. 476 I CCC, the reuse means the intention of the user to use the contract terms for at least two contracts is sufficient, but this means little in practice. The more important information expressed in the wording is that B2C contracts are exempted from this precondition of reuse, but this exemption makes almost no sense in practice since the Chinese courts usually also base their determination of reuse on appearance rather than intention.

2.1.2.1 The Intention of Reuse

There were controversies about whether the intention of reuse should be one of the elements to define standard business terms. There were opinions of Chinese scholars calling for the Chinese legislator not to set this precondition.[29] However, the legislator holds that the intention of reuse is a particular feature of standard business terms and it would therefore cause legal uncertainty if the determination of standard business terms relied solely on whether a contractual term had been negotiated, without the observation of whether it was intended to be reused.[30] The precondition of reuse requires the contractual partner to prove that the user has the intention of reuse, regardless of how many times the user has actually used them.[31] Therefore, the implication of the Chinese legislator setting

27 See BGH NJW 1991, 843 (843); BGH ZIP 2005, 1604 (1604).
28 OLG Düsseldorf NJW-RR 1997, 1147; MüKoBGB/Basedow BGB § 305, Rn. 18.
29 See WANG Liming, p. 405 （王利明：《合同法研究》，中国人民大学出版社2015年版，第405页）.
30 HUANG Wei, p. 953.
31 HUANG Wei, p. 953.

the precondition of the intention of reuse, is the same as the usual understanding of § 305 I BGB: if the user has an intention to reuse, the contractual terms are already standard business terms when they are used for the first time. What is different, however, is that the requirement of at least three uses of the contract terms under § 305 I BGB does not exist in the Chinese Civil Code. This distinction is also the consequence of differences in the wording between the "multiple-use" in § 305 I BGB and the "reuse" in Art. 496 I CCC.

2.1.2.2 The Appearance of Contractual Terms

In Chinese judicial practice, the courts will determine that the contractual terms are intended for reuse when they are the same in several different contracts in terms of structure and content.[32] To prove the purpose of reuse can also be to examine whether the content of the contractual terms is the same as the contract sample unilaterally drafted by the user or the third party.[33]

For B2C standard business terms, the courts will often even take the appearance as the sole criterion for the intention of reuse and not systematically examine whether or not the user had the intention of using the contractual terms in question repeatedly.[34] However, the courts do not specify that this path for the determination of the intention of reuse is only applicable to B2C contracts. That means, at least theoretically, that the above-mentioned determination of the intention of reuse based on appearance is applicable to both B2C and B2B contracts.

The judicial determination of the intention of reuse based on appearance is only an exception for B2B contracts. In principle, even though B2B contractual terms are obviously the same in terms of structure and content as other transactions, a special background of the transaction can be used to deny the intention of reuse.[35] Only where the content of the contract is relatively simple,

32 The Chinese Supreme Court (2013) minti 216 (最高人民法院民事判决书(2013)民提字第216号).

33 The Chinese Supreme Court (2018) minshen 6080 (最高人民法院民事裁定书(2018)最高法民申6080号).

34 See the Chinese Supreme Court (2019) minzai 608 (最高人民法院民事判决书（2019）最高法民再245号).

35 See the Chinese Supreme Court (2018) minzai 413 (最高人民法院民事判决书(2018)最高法民再413号); the Beijing Third Intermediate Court (2021) jing 03 minzhong 3482 (北京市第三中级人民法院(2021)京03民终3482号民事判决书); the Hebei Higher Court (2018) jiminchu114 (河北省高级人民法院民事判决书(2018)冀民初114号).

and the appearance shows an obvious feature of reuse, the Chinese courts will apply the above determination of the intention of reuse based on appearance, to B2B contracts.[36] Unfortunately, the Chinese courts never illustrate or enumerate the special backgrounds that are eligible to deny the intention of reuse. The use of special backgrounds, therefore, has no regular pattern.

Generally, the significantly weakened role of the appearance of the contract in the determination of standard business terms, makes the B2B contractual terms far more difficult to qualify as standard business terms in Chinese judicial practice. That leads to the significantly weaker control of standard business terms in the B2B field because it is much easier for the Chinese courts to consider the B2B contractual terms as individually negotiated terms than for the German courts.

In summary, the difference in the textual meanings between the reuse precondition in Art. 496 I CCC and the multiple-use precondition in § 305 I BGB has little influence in practice. Both the Chinese courts and the German courts base their determination of the intention of reuse or multiple-use mainly on the appearance of contractual terms. The main difference between China and Germany is in their handling of B2B contracts. Although the Chinese courts do not rule out the determination of the intention of reuse based on the appearance for B2B contracts, they often use special backgrounds of transactions to deny the existence of the intention of reuse in the B2B field. That makes it easier for B2B contractual terms to be considered as individually negotiated terms in Chinese judicial practice than those in German legal practice.

2.2 Pre-Formulation

2.2.1 The Unilateral Pre-Formulation in § 305 I BGB

A contractual term is unilaterally pre-formulated if it is drafted by one party (the user) in anticipatory preparation of the conclusion of a contract without a specific contractual negotiation with the other party to the contract (the contractual partner).[37] Standard business terms are not necessarily drafted by the user though but may also be drafted by a third party selected by the user.[38] Unilateral pre-formulation of standard business terms is closely connected with the intention of multiple-use. Thus, except for consumer contracts (§ 310 III Nr. 2 BGB),

---

36 See the Geizhou Zuiyi Intermediate Court (2020) qian 03 minzhong 1531(贵州省遵义市中级人民法院民事判决书(2020)黔03民终1531号).

37 BeckOGK/Lehmann-Richter § 305, Rn. 107; Staudinger/Mäsch § 305, Rn. 25.

38 BGH NJW 1984, 360.

the first draft of a contract by one party for the specific party to the contract is not unilateral pre-formulation in the sense of § 305 I 1 BGB.[39] There are two perspectives to determine the unilateral pre-formulation of a contract. The macro determination of pre-formulation is based on the complete text of the contract.[40] The micro determination of pre-formulation focuses on a single contractual term.[41] Contractual terms in need of supplements and contractual terms with multiple options are special cases of the unilateral pre-formulation.

2.2.1.1 Contractual Terms in Need of Supplements

If a contractual term has to be supplemented with more information by the contractual partner, it will be a standard business term unless this information is an independent supplement.[42] That means a contractual term is a standard business term if it contains the content to be judicially checked in itself and this contractual term only needs to be completed by dependent supplements specifying the subject matter of the contract in individual cases.[43]

In contrast, an independent supplement has an influence on the substantive content of the contractual term.[44] A contractual term needing independent supplements is not an individually negotiated term unless the contractual partner makes a decision about the contract freely.[45]

German practice of applying the micro determination perspective of standard business terms.

2.2.1.2 Contractual Terms with Multiple Options

Another example of this micro perspective is a contractual term with multiple options for the contractual partner. The differentiation between dependence and independence also applies here. The principle is that if the contractual partner has the opportunity to make his own choice independently from the user and if he makes use of this opportunity, the contractual term should be an individually negotiated term.[46] According to this principle, a contractual term with options

---

39 BGH 1974, 37 f. Ulmer/Habersack § 305, Rn. 22.

40 z.B. BGH NJW 2000, 1110 (1111); OLG Düsseldorf NZG 1998, 352; OLG Dresden BB 1999, 228.

41 Cf. BGH NJW 1997, 135 f; OLG Rostock BauR 2005, 1037.

42 z.B. BGH NJW 2014, 2940 Rn. 17; also MüKoBGB/Basedow BGB § 305 Rn. 15.

43 Cf. BGH NJW 1987, 1636; 1998, 2815; 2010, 3431 Rn. 16; 2018, 2950 Rn. 31.

44 Cf. BGH NJW 2003, 1313, 1314; NJW 1982, 1035; NJW 1992, 746.

45 BGH NJW 1988, 1066 (1067).

46 BGHZ 153, 148(151); BGH NJW 2008, 987 Rn. 21.

is an individually negotiated term if the user allows its contractual partner to formulate and supplement his own specific option to this contractual term away from the options provided by the user in advance.[47] For the determination of an individually negotiated term, it is not sufficient that the contractual partner is allowed to choose different contractual terms with different prices. This is unless the user has access to negotiations, in which at least one of the options is to change the ratio between obligations and remuneration.[48] That also applies to B2B contracts.[49] Therefore, it is not an individually negotiated term, for example, if an airline company gives the traveler the choice of either waiving his legal right of withdrawal or paying a higher tariff.[50]

2.2.2 The Pre-Formulation in Art. 496 I CCC

In Art. 496 I CCC, pre-formulation is also one of the constituent preconditions of standard business terms. According to the literal meaning of Art. 496 I CCC, the party to a contract who pre-formulates standard business terms should be the user, if strictly interpreted. However, in Chinese civil law theory, a standard business term under Art. 496 I CCC can also be pre-formulated by a third party.[51]

In Chinese judicial practice concerning B2C contracts, when a contract has a unilaterally drafted appearance, especially if it is printed in advance or electronically presented, it will be easily recognized by the Chinese courts as having standard business terms.[52] That also applies to B2B contracts in some cases, for example, a B2B contract on the delivery service of an ordinary parcel.[53]

In principle, in Chinese judicial practice, B2B contracts are usually subject to higher requirements for the recognition of standard business terms

---

47 Cf. BGH NJW-RR 2018, 814 (815); BGH VersR 1996, 741; BGH NJW 1998, 1066.

48 BGH NJW 1988, 410; Ulmer/Habersac § 305, Rn. 53 f.

49 Cf. BGH NJW 2017, 2346; BGH NJW-RR 2018, 814.

50 BeckOGK/Lehmann-Richter § 305, Rn. 169; AG Köln NJW 2017, 2047.

51 SU Haopeng, S. 149.

52 See The Guangdong Guangzhong Intermediate Court (2016) yue 01 minzhong 2343 (广东省广州市中级人民法院民事判决书(2016)粤01民终2343号); The Henan Zhumadian Intermediate Court (2015) zhuminyizhongzi 00648 (河南省驻马店市中级人民法院民事判决书(2015)驻民一终字第00648号); The Guangdong Zhongshan First Court (2019) yuemin 2071 minshen 32 (广东省中山市第一人民法院(2019)粤2071民申32号民事裁定书).

53 The Beijing Third Intermediate Court (2021) jing 03 minzhong 3482 (北京市第三中级人民法院(2021)京03民终3482号民事判决书).

in complicated contracts such as contracts on the bidding of infrastructure projects.[54] When a B2B contractual term has information to be supplemented, Chinese courts generally determine that the contractual term is not a standard business term.[55] Similarly, if there are multiple options in a B2B contractual term, Chinese courts generally consider it to be an individually negotiated term rather than a standard business term.[56]

The Chinese courts adopt these relatively loose criteria for an individually negotiated term because this approach makes the control of B2B standard business terms weaker. A contractual term would be exempted from Art. 497 CCC if the courts determine it not to be a standard business term. And multiple options create a possibility for the contractual partner to choose the content of contractual terms before the contractual conclusion. That gives Chinese courts an excuse not to apply the stricter Art. 497 CCC, according to which nearly all B2B the standard business terms with a negative effect to the contractual partner are likely to be invalid. However, Chinese courts do not illustrate whether and why the looser criteria mentioned above are exclusively applicable to B2B contracts, creating legal uncertainty for the control of standard business terms.

2.3 Negotiation (Aushandeln)

2.3.1 Negotiation in § 305 I BGB

In § 305 I BGB, the negotiation (Aushandeln) is the key precondition used to distinguish standard business terms from individually negotiated terms. Determining whether the parties to the contract have negotiated the terms, is decisive to whether they are subject to the control of the standard business terms.

2.3.1.1 The Negotiation in the Interpretation of the BGH

According to German case law, the "negotiation" precondition in § 305 I BGB requires that the user should make the content of the non-legal core content of the contractual terms available to their contractual partner for revisions if necessary. In other words, the content amending or supplementing essential content of legal rules should be available to the contractual partner who should be

54 Tibet Rike Intermediate Court (2021) zhang 02 minzhong 7 (西藏自治区日喀则市中级人民法院民事判决书(2021)藏02民终7号).

55 Jiangsu Nantong Intermediate Court (2020) su 06 minzhong 2747 (江苏省南通市中级人民法院民事判决书(2020)苏06民终2747号).

56 Chongqing Higher Court (2021) yuminzhong 32 (重庆市高级人民法院民事裁定书(2021)渝民辖终32号).

free to actively influence the design of these contractual terms.[57] Even for a B2B contract, the mere willingness of the user to negotiate the contractual terms is not sufficient for them to be individually negotiated terms.[58]

The German Federal Court of Justice (der Bundesgerichtshof in German, hereafter abbreviated as BGH) where necessary stated that the negotiation (Aushandeln) in § 305 I 3 BGB means more than a pure negotiation (Verhandeln).[59] In order to make pre-formulated contractual terms negotiated according to the meaning of § 305 I 3 BGB, the user of the contractual terms must clearly and seriously declare to the contractual partner that they are ready to change each of these contractual terms.[60] The contractual partner should have, at the very least, a real chance to influence the content of the contractual conditions.[61]

The BGH grants the "negotiation" precondition of § 305 I BGB a more complicated meaning than its normal meaning. According to this more complicated meaning, the readiness of the user to change any of the pre-formulated contractual terms is the core idea of the "negotiation" precondition.

2.3.1.2 Change of Content as a Regular Result of Negotiation

If the standard business terms remain unchanged, the interests of the user are unilaterally safeguarded and there are significant deviations from legal regulations that are intended to protect the legitimate interests of the customer, then there is no negotiation within the meaning of § 305 I 3 BGB according to BGH.[62] The BGH only permits under special circumstances that an unchanged pre-formulated contractual term can be assessed as the result of a negotiation. A pre-formulated contractual term is exceptionally an individually negotiated contractual term only if it ultimately remains the same after the proposed draft is thoroughly discussed between the two sides.[63] This principle is also generally applicable to B2B transactions[64] and is therefore strongly criticized.[65]

---

57 BGH NJW 1991, 1678; 1992, 2283; BGH 143; 103; NJW 2005, 1805; NJW-RR 2009, 947 Rn. 15; NJW 2013, 856 Rn. 10.

58 Cf. BGH NJW-RR 1986, 54; BGH NZBau 2016, 213 Rn. 26.

59 BGHZ 153, 311 (321); NJW-RR 2005, 1040; NJW 2013, 856; OLG Köln WM 2002, 853 ff.; OLG Schleswig MDR 1991, 262; OLG Hamm NJW-RR 2002, 1487.

60 BGH NJW-RR 2018, 814 (815).

61 BGH NJW 2005, 2543 (2544); BGH NJW 2013, 856 (858); BGH NJW 2014, 1725 (1727); BGH NJW 2016, 1230 (1232).

62 Cf. BGH NJW 1981, 2343; Peters NJW 1982, 562.

63 BGH NJW 1998, 2600 (2601); BGH 204, 346 Rn. 33.

64 BGH NJW 1988, 140; 2013, 856 Rn 10; 2013, 2027 Rn. 20; 206, 305.

65 Z.B. Lischek/Mahnken, ZIP 2007, 158 (160); Berger NJW 2010, 465 (465).

It cannot be denied that a change of content is the easiest condition to identify in order to prove the existence of a negotiation. The adoption of this condition to determine a negotiation makes it easy for the German courts to grant a high degree of protection to the contractual partner, which may not be totally suitable for all B2B transactions.[66] More detailed discussions should be had on the relationship between changes of content and negotiations in order to differentiate between B2B and B2C contracts.

2.3.1.3 The Micro Perspective Through the Word "soweit"

In the opinion of the BGH, the assessment of whether the contractual conditions were unilaterally designed or individually negotiated should be made in relation to every individual contractual term and not in relation to the entire contract (a micro angle of view).[67] By interpreting the word "soweit" ("as long as" in English) from § 305 I 3 BGB, the BGH believes that other unilaterally drafted contractual terms in the same contract are still standard business terms in principle even if some contractual terms in this contract have already become individually negotiated terms through negotiations.[68] However, there is also a German judicial opinion that proposes to establish an exception: if a number of terms in a contract have been changed by negotiations, especially concerning important points within the contract, and every term that remains unchanged has actually been included in the negotiation process, the entire contract should be viewed as negotiated.[69] It remains to be clarified further though, which terms in a contract are "important points" and how to determine whether every unchanged term has actually been included in the negotiation process.

Despite these questions, the macro perspective is still necessary since the micro point of view is too high of a requirement for B2B contracts and does not conform to the practice of many B2B transactions where the parties to the contract could focus themselves just on the negotiation of some contractual terms in the process of private autonomy.

An academic opinion is meaningful for determining the connection between the micro and macro angle. According to academic understandings, changes in some pre-formulated contractual terms indicate the negotiation of the entire

---

66 See Chapter 4, part 3.1 and part 3.2.1.1 of this dissertation.

67 BGH NJW 2014, 1725 Rn. 27; 2003, 1805 (1807).

68 BGH 97 215, BGH NJW 83, 1603, BGH 98, 3488; BGH NJW 2000, 1110 (1111); ZIP 1996, 1997; Düsseldorf BB 1997, 598; Palandt/Grüneberg BGB § 305, Rn. 18.

69 Hamm WM 1989, 1016.

contract that comprises formal standard terms.[70] The prerequisite for this indication is, firstly, that the unchanged terms are formulated in a clear and understandable way by one party and secondly, that the other party has been informed in detail about their content and legal implications.[71] In addition, however, the customer must know or have known that there is a connection between the unchanged contractual terms and the outcome of the negotiations on the changed contractual terms, which justifies the assumption that the unchanged terms were the subject of the negotiations.[72]

The additional meaning of the word "soweit" limits negotiations to each contractual term. This judicial practice is not suitable for B2B contracts and should be revised to this extent.[73]

2.3.1.4 Material Negotiations Instead of Formal Discussions

According to § 305 I S. 3 BGB, there is no negotiation if the contractual partner is given the choice of either accepting the conditions unchanged or refusing to conclude the contract.[74] Even if the user of the pre-formulated contractual text reads out the contract to the contractual partner, explains the text to them, or discusses the text with the contractual partner, it does not constitute a negotiation in line with 305 I 3 BGB according to the BGH.[75] An exception to this usual criterion happens when the user makes his terms and conditions available to the contractual partner for possible changes, but the contractual partner decides to accept these contractual terms unchanged based on the belief of their necessity or for a lower price.[76] All above practice means the BGH requires strict material negotiations rather than formal discussions as the precondition for one-side drafted terms and conditions to be considered individually negotiated contractual terms.

2.3.1.5 The Burden of Persuasion and Proof

In proving the presence of material negotiations, the burden of persuasion and proof is important. All circumstances in individual cases must be taken into

70 MüKoBGB /Basedow BGB § 305 Rn. 39.
71 BGH NJW 2005, 2543 (2544).
72 MüKoBGB / Basedow BGB § 305 Rn. 41.
73 Huth, S. 100.
74 BGH NJW 1991, 1678; 1992, 1107.
75 BGH 104, 232; NJW 1988, 410; 1991, 1678; 1992, 2759; WM 1995, 1455; NJW 2005, 1574.
76 BGH NJW 1991, 1678; 1998, 2600; 2000, 1110; Stuttgart WM 2002, 667.

account in order to judge the existence of a negotiation.[77] The user bears the burden of persuasion and proof.[78] In B2B cases too, the user always bears the burden of persuasion and proof that a contractual term has been changed at the request of the contractual partner.[79] Even if the terms and conditions have been introduced into an earlier individually negotiated contract, the user also has to prove the material negotiation before the conclusion of a new contract.[80]

This burden of persuasion and proof is not applied differently between B2B and B2C contracts and is too strict to the control in the B2B field.

2.3.1.6 The Same Rules Regulating B2C Contracts and B2B Contracts

The above criteria used to judge whether a standard business term is negotiated are nearly the same for both B2B contracts and B2C contracts.[81]

There are various cases which illustrate their equal treatment further. Even if the user and the B2B contractual partner agree on a protocol for negotiations and the contractual terms have been negotiated according to this protocol, it is not sufficient for the determination of a negotiation.[82] It is also not considered to be a negotiation if the user has reached an agreement with the contractual partner that the concluded contract has been "negotiated seriously and extensively."[83] According to the BGH, there is also no negotiation in the B2B field even if the contract draft with the standard business terms has been sent to the contractual partner with the request for comments or changes.[84] Neither is a lengthy discussion on the B2B terms and conditions sufficient to qualify them as negotiations.[85]

These obviously strict cases for B2B contracts can persuade us that a differentiation between the B2B and B2C is needed.

2.3.2 Negotiation in Art. 496 I CCC

Like the situation in Germany, a negotiation within the meaning of Art. 496 I CCC is also one of the main elements for the determination of standard

---

77 BGH 206, 305 Rn. 23.
78 BGH NJW 1998, 2600;1998, 3488.
79 BGH ZIP 2014, 924.
80 BGH WM 1978, 1384; Hamm NJW-RR 1987, 243.
81 Cf. BGH 143, 103; NJW 2003, 1805; BGH 200, 326 Rn. 28.
82 BGHZ 200, 326 = NJW 2014, 1725 Rn. 27; BGH NZBau 2016, 213 Rn. 25.
83 BGH ZIP 2014, 924.
84 BGH ZIP 2016, 474.
85 BGH NJW 2013, 856; BGH ZIP 1987, 1576 = NJW 1988, 410, 411.

business terms. Also similar to the German Civil Code, in Chinese there are words for Verhandeln and Aushandeln. These words correspond to cuoshang (磋商) and xieshang (协商) in Chinese respectively. But unlike German civil law practice and academic discussions, the distinction between cuoshang (磋商) and xieshang (协商) is rarely involved in the practice of and academic discussions over Art. 496 I CCC in China. That means the determination of negotiations in Art. 496 I CCC is not connected to the semantic difference between cuoshang and xieshang in Chinese.

2.3.2.1 The Looser Tendency in the Determination of Negotiations of B2B Contracts and its Lack of Legal Certainty

Unlike the German Civil Code, the Chinese courts' approach to determining a negotiation of a B2B contract is in principle looser than that of B2C contracts. An extreme example is when there is a declaration in a B2B contract that "the two parties conclude this contract after negotiations." Here, it is possible for a Chinese court to rule that the parties negotiated all the terms in the contract before the conclusion without an examination into whether this declaration was actually a standard business term even if this statement "after negotiations" comes as a rather standard phrase.[86] In B2C contracts, the determination of negotiation is much stricter, and this kind of declaration usually is not sufficient for the determination of negotiations.[87]

In addition to the extreme example above, a formally free decision made by the contractual partner for the conclusion of a contract is one of the core ideas for judging whether there is a negotiation. A method for determining an individually negotiated term under this criterion is that there is no standard business term where the contractual partner is deemed to have the ability to choose a contract or negotiate it.[88] Another implication of this criterion of whether a contract was negotiated, relies on whether the contractual partner to the contract

86 See the Supreme Court (2015) minerzhong 381 (最高人民法院民事裁定书(2015)民二终字第381号); the Supreme Court (2018) minxiazhong 355 (最高人民法院民事裁定书(2018)最高法民辖终355号).

87 See The Supreme Court (2015) minzai 245 (最高人民法院民事判决书（2019）最高法民再245号).

88 See The Hubei Ezhou Intermediate Court (2021) e 07 minzhong 388 (湖北省鄂州市中级人民法院民事判决书(2021)鄂07民终388号).

had the freedom to refuse or to conclude the contract.[89] However, the freedom to refuse the conclusion of the contract and the freedom to negotiate the contract are distinct from one another, yet the Chinese courts do not seem to consider this difference in many B2B cases. It cannot be denied that the Chinese courts adopt a looser approach to determining the presence of a negotiation in B2B contracts as the above two approaches are not frequently used in B2C contracts. In B2C contracts, the formal appearance of the agreement often amounts to not only the presumption of the intention of reuse, but even a presumption of the existence of standard business terms. There are often no further checks into whether the contractual partner had the freedom to refuse or negotiate a contract.

However, this looser approach of the Chinese courts' in the B2B field lacks legal certainty. The courts have never specified in their decisions whether the above approaches are only applicable to B2B contracts or also to B2C contracts. This legal uncertainty has meant that there are B2C judicial cases where the courts have determined a negotiation within a B2C contract based on the argument that the consumer had the freedom to refuse the conclusion of the contract.[90] This legal uncertainty also manifests itself in various B2B cases where the courts have declared the existence of standard business terms based only on the appearance of the contract.[91]

Chinese practical judicial cases show a tendency to treat B2B and B2C contracts differently although this tendency is not visible in all cases.[92] The preconditions for exceptions also remain unclear.

2.3.2.2 The Introduction of Factors in the Background of Transactions

In order to differentiate between individually negotiated terms and standard business terms, some Chinese courts consider factors in transactions to be relevant, and rely on, for instance, whether the contractual partner has the "right to an equal negotiation." Considering the factors in transactions means that "it is necessary to consider whether the user has a monopoly in the industry and

---

89 See The Supreme Court (2017) minzhong 91 (最高人民法院(2017) 最高法民终 91 号民事裁定书); The Supreme Court (2017) minshen2136 (最高人民法院(2017) 最高法民申 2136 号民事裁定书).

90 For example Fujian Higher Court (2017) minminshen 692 (福建省高级人民法院民事裁定书（2017）闽民申692号).

91 For example The Supreme Court (2013) mintizi 216 (最高人民法院民事判决书(2013)民提字第216号).

92 For example see the Supreme Court (2020) zuigaofaminshen 2963 (最高人民法院民事裁定书(2020)最高法民申2963号).

whether the contractual partner has the ability to identify business risks and to introduce a negotiation in order to judge the existence of this right to equal negotiations."[93] In other words, even if a contractual term is unilaterally pre-formulated and reused, and the two parties have never discussed this contract term, this contractual term should also be regarded as an individually negotiated term when the aforementioned circumstances are satisfied. Like the other looser approaches to determine negotiations, this approach concerning the "right to an equal negotiation" does not mention whether it is specific to B2B transactions—although judicial cases applying this approach have only involved B2B contracts. The deficit of this approach stands that the courts have never given concrete criteria to check whether the factors are satisfied. For example, it is unclear under what circumstances the contractual partner would have the ability to identify business risks and the ability for negotiations, and thus this approach lacks legal certainty.

Unlike German courts, Chinese courts make endeavors to adopt different approaches to judge negotiations between B2B transactions and B2C transactions, but each of the above-mentioned approaches lack legal certainty and do not clearly relate themselves to the differentiation between B2B and B2C transactions. This is probably because the non-differentiation between B2B and B2C transactions in the Chinese legislation restricts the freedom of the courts' arguments. Therefore, a systematic approach to this differentiation on the issue of the determination of negotiations is also needed in Chinese law, just as it is needed in German law.

2.4 Summary

The above comparison between China and Germany on the definition of standard business terms provides an understanding of their similarities, differences, and their respective deficits. The German precondition of "multiple-use" is almost the same as the Chinese precondition of "reuse." Contrarily, the determinations of the "pre-formulation" and the "negotiation" between German law and the Chinese law are very different. The most important issue on these differences is the differentiation between B2B and B2C contracts. The respective deficits of Chinese law and German law manifest themselves on this issue. German law and courts apply the same criteria for the "pre-formulation" and the "negotiation" to both B2C and B2B contractual terms, which impose excessive control

93 See Jiangsu Higher Court (2016) suminshen 612 (江苏省高级人民法院民事裁定书(2016)苏民申612号).

over B2B contracts. Chinese courts make use of the "pre-formulation" and the "negotiation" in order to exclude some B2B standard business terms from this control but such practices lack strong arguments and legal certainty. Therefore, an appropriate approach to the differentiation between B2B and B2C contracts in the determination of standard business terms remains a central discussion.[94]

3 Incorporation Control: § 305 II BGB and Art. 496 II CCC

Although both the German Civil Code and the Chinese Civil Code have legislative regulations concerning incorporation control, their content and scope of application differ from each other. Incorporation control is still new and faces a lot of uncertainty in China. The relevant German experience, therefore, can be very useful for the interpretation and application of incorporation control.

§ 305 II BGB and Art. 496 II CCC are as follows:

> § 305 II BGB:
> "Standard business terms only become a part of a contract if the user, when entering into the contract,
> 1. reminds the other party to the contract of them explicitly or, where explicit reminder, due to the way in which the contract is entered into, is possible only with disproportionate difficulty, by posting a clearly visible notice at the place where the contract is entered into, and
> 2. gives the other party to the contract, in an acceptable manner, which also takes into reasonable account any physical handicap of the other party to the contract that is discernible to the user, the opportunity to take notice of their contents,
> and if the other party to the contract agrees to their applying."
> Art. 496 II CCC:
> "Upon concluding a contract, where a standard business term is used, the party providing the standard clause shall determine the parties' rights and obligations in accordance with the principle of fairness, and shall, in a reasonable manner, draw the other party's (the contractual partner's) attention to the term concerning the other party's major interests, such as a term that exempts or alleviates the liability of the party providing the standard clause (the user), and give explanations of such term upon request of the other party. Where the party providing the standard clause fails to perform the aforementioned obligation of drawing attention or giving explanations, thus resulting in the other party's failure to pay attention to or understand the clause concerning his major interests, the other party may claim that such term does not become part of the contract."

94 See Chapter 4, part 3.2.1.1 and 3.2.2.1 of this dissertation.

3.1 Incorporation Control in § 305 II BGB

According to § 310 I BGB, § 305 II BGB is not applicable to B2B contracts. This is one of the important regulatory distinctions between B2B and B2C standard business terms in the German Civil Code.

Because standard business terms are not individually negotiated like normal contractual terms, special legal requirements are set up for their effective incorporation by § 305 II BGB, which are much stricter than the general contract law.[95] These requirements modify general contract law.[96] These special legal modifications include the requirement of an explicit reminder of the standard business terms, an acceptable opportunity to take note of the content of the standard business terms, and a consent to the standard business terms.

3.1.1 The Explicit Reminder

§ 305 BGB restricts the possibility of implied contractual incorporation at the meaning of § § 133, 157 BGB because an explicit reminder of the standard business terms is required from the user before the conclusion of the contract.[97] The explicit reminder must include all standard business terms.[98] This is very different from the requirements in Art. 496 II CCC.

A specification as to the form of the reminder is not prescribed.[99] What is necessary is a clear, unmistakable, and conspicuous reminder.[100] In most cases, it should be expressed by words instead of behavior.[101] An Implied behavior, for example, simply providing the standard business terms, is not sufficient.[102]

3.1.1.1 A Standard Contract: The Most Common but Simplest Case

A standard contract is one of the usual forms of standard business terms, and the requirement of the reminder is easily satisfied in this case because all standard business terms applicable to the contract are already included in its text. If the contract is signed by the contractual partner, there is no obligation of the user

95 Cf. UBH/Ulmer/Habersack § 305 BGB Rn 118; Erman/Roloff/Looschelders § 305 BGB, Rn. 25.
96 Cf. UBH /Ulmer/ Habersack § 305 BGB Rn 118; Staudinger/Mäsch § 305 BGB Rn. 9.
97 BGH NJW-RR 1987 112(113); Pffeifer § 305, Rn. 66.
98 Wolf/Pffeifer § 305 BGB Rn. 68.
99 BGH NJW 1983, 816.
100 BGH ZIP 1981, 1221.
101 Staudinger/ Mäsch § 305 BGB, Rn. 111; For exceptions, BGH NJW-RR 1987, 112.
102 BGH ZIP 1986, 1126; NJW-RR 1987, 112.

to additionally draw the contractual partner's attention to the standard business terms already formally included in the contract text.[103]

Incorporation control in § 305 II BGB has no great meaning to standard contracts. A standard contract is not the main object regulated by § 305 II BGB. This is quite different from Art. 497 II CCC, where a standard contract is considered to be one of the most important objects of incorporation control.

3.1.1.2 A Clear, Concrete and Not-to-Be-Neglected Reminder

Printed standard business terms on the back of an offer letter are to be differentiated from standard contracts. If there is no corresponding note on the front, it is not sufficient as a reminder[104] because the standard business terms could be neglected. Similarly, even the printing of the standard business terms in brochures, catalogs, price lists, or other documents is not able to replace an explicit reminder.[105]

According to § 305 II Nr. 1 BGB, if an explicit reminder is too difficult to be made due to disproportionate difficulties as a result of the nature of the contract, a clearly visible notice at the place where the contract is to be concluded is sufficient and valid for the same purposes as an explicit reminder. This ensures that German law does not ignore the contracts of daily life, in which an explicit reminder sometimes is only possible with great effort and expense,[106] for example, the contracts concerning the use of lockers.[107]

The core idea of these rules, established through German case law, over the explicit reminder is to inform the contractual partner of the standard business terms. These requirements make it possible for the contractual partner to know that there will be standard business terms as part of the contract to be concluded.

3.1.2 The Opportunity in an Acceptable Manner to Take Note of the Content

The opportunity in an acceptable manner to take note of the content of standard business terms written in § 305 II Nr. 2 BGB means that the user must ensure that the contractual partner is given access to the full text of the standard

103 BGH NJW 1995, 190.

104 BGH WM 1983, 269; ZIP 1986, 1126; Köln NJW-RR 1987, 53; Nürnberg WM 1990, 1370.

105 LG Berlin BB 1980, 1770.

106 BT-Drs. 7/3919, 18.

107 LG Essen VersR 1995, 1198.

business terms before making a decision about the conclusion of the contract and is not forced to either accept the standard business terms unseen or to forfeit the conclusion of the contract.[108]

It is irrelevant whether the contractual partner makes use of this opportunity or not.[109] It is usually sufficient that the standard business terms are physically handed to the contractual partner or, in an online transaction, that the user offers them to the contractual partner with a link to be clicked with the possibility to print them.[110] Only if the user can expect with certainty that the contractual partner is already familiar with the relevant standard business terms, there is an exception to ease the above requirements, which must also be strictly applied in the interests of the contractual partner.[111] It is not sufficient if the contractual partner only gets access to the content of the disadvantageous terms and conditions while the other standard business terms are not referred to by the user.[112]

3.1.2.1 Readability and Comprehensibility

This opportunity also requires the readability and comprehensibility of the standard business terms.[113] Standard business terms should be legible to the naked eye without difficulty.[114] In the absence of sufficient comprehensibility, standard business terms are excluded from incorporation into the contract.[115]

3.1.3 The Declaration of Consent

The declaration of consent does not need to be specifically proven for every individual standard business term. It is sufficient if the declaration of consent is entirely oriented toward all standard business terms generally.[116] This is justified

108 Cf. BGH 1994, 2547; MDR 1999, 1061; Erman/Roloff/Looschelders § 305 BGB, Rn. 33; Bamberger/Roth/Becker BGB § 305 Rn. 56.
109 BGH NJW 2002, 370 (372).
110 Bamberger/Roth/Becker BGB § 305 Rn. 58.
111 BGH 86, 135; 105, 290; BGHZ 109,184 ff. = NJW 1990, 715; Erman/Roloff/Looschelders § 305 BGB, Rn. 33.
112 BGH NJW-RR 1991, (727); Erman/Roloff/Looschelders § 305 BGB, Rn. 33; cf. Bamberger/Roth/Becker BGB § 305 Rn. 53.
113 Berger/Roth/Becker BGB § 305 Rn. 58.
114 BGH NJW 1983, 2772; Saarbrücken NJW-RR 1988, 858; LG München VuR 1996, 36; Staudinger /Mäsch § 305 BGB Rn. 140.
115 BGH NJW 1981, 867; Schleswig NJW 1995, 2858.
116 Cf. Erman/Roloff/Looschelders § 305 BGB, Rn. 41.

because according to § 305 II Nr. 1 and Nr. 2, a reasonable reminder and an opportunity to take note of each standard business term must already have been given to the contractual partner, and it is left to the contractual partner whether he or she acts on this.[117] The only exception is that the declaration does not extend to surprising terms (§ 305c I BGB).[118]

In summary of the German law concerning incorporation control in § 305 II BGB, we can see very strict requirements in order for standard business terms to be incorporated into the contract. The core idea of incorporation control is to provide the contractual partner enough chances to get access to and understand the standard business terms as the essential preconditions to accepting these terms as part of the contract. It is unsurprising that these requirements are not applicable to B2B contracts, where B2B contractual partners are certainly expected to be given access to the standard business terms and understand them actively even without these legal preconditions.

3.2 Incorporation Control in Art. 496 II CCC

"Incorporation control" is new terminology in Chinese civil law. Although Art. 39 I CCL stipulated that the user should draw the other party's attention to the standard business terms in a reasonable manner that exempt or limit its liability, and should explain them in accordance with the requirements of the contractual partner, this provision does not stipulate any legal consequences in breach of the requirements. Therefore, there was a dispute over whether there truly is incorporation control in Chinese law.[119] At the end, Art. 496 II CCC adds that the other party is entitled to claim that the standard business term should not be part of the contract if the user has not performed the obligation of drawing attention to or explaining the standard business term, and as a result the contractual party did not pay attention to or understand a standard business term with major interests of the contractual partner.

3.2.1 Incorporation Control Both for B2C Contracts and B2B Contracts

Art. 496 II CCC is the legal basis of incorporation control in the Chinese Civil Code. Art. 496 II CCC is enacted based on Art. 39 I CCL. Art. 26 I of the Chinese

117 Cf. BGH 86, 135.

118 Wolf/ Pfeiffer, § 305 BGB Rn. 104.

119 CUI Jianyuan, QFX 2014, no. 6, p. 53 (崔建远:《编纂民法典必须摆正几对关系》,《清华法学》2014 年第 6 期); WANG Liming, FSYJ 1994, no. 3, p. 9 (王利明:《对〈合同法〉格式条款 规定的评析》,《政法论坛》1999 年第 6 期).

Consumer Rights and Interests Protection Law (CRIPL) also stipulates incorporation control. Art. 26 I CRIPL expands the scope of incorporation control compared with Art. 39 I CCL. The drawing attention and explanations in the CRIPL are also applicable to the standard business terms on "the quantity and quality of goods or services, the prices or expenses, performance deadlines and methods, safety precautions and risk warnings, after-sales service, civil liability and other content with a major interest of consumers." Similarly, Art. 496 II CCC also expands the scope of incorporation control compared with Art. 39 I CCL and summarizes the standard business terms in the scope of incorporation control as "contents that have a major interest of the contractual partner", the scope of which is very close to Art. 26 I CRIPL. As a result, it is difficult to distinguish Art. 496 II CCC and Art. 26 I CRIPL from each other.

That means the B2B and B2C standard business terms are both subject to incorporation control of Chinese law. This is the most significant difference in terms of incorporation control between Chinese law and German law. What should not be ignored, is that there are in fact significant differences over the elements of incorporation control within Chinese and German law, which will be discussed later in this dissertation.[120]

What should also be noted, is that although the Chinese Contract Law and its related judicial interpretations lost their legal validity after the Chinese Civil Code came into effect, Art. 496 II CCC retains the same terminology that should be understood consistently with Art. 39 I CCL. Therefore, the judicial interpretation of the Chinese Contract Law by the Supreme Court of China still plays an important role in academic discussions and judicial practice concerning Art. 496 II CCC before new judicial interpretations come about.

3.2.2 *Special Marks to Draw the Contractual Partner's Attention*

Art. 6 of the Second Interpretation on Several Issues Concerning the Application of the Contract Law of the People's Republic of China is one key judicial interpretation of the Chinese Contract Law of the Supreme Court. It states that it is enough to meet the requirement of drawing the attention of the contractual partner to the standard business terms excluding or restricting the liability of the user in a reasonable manner prescribed by Art. 39 CCL if the user of the standard business terms uses special signs such as words, symbols, fonts, etc. to mark the standard business terms excluding or restricting the liability of the user. This judicial interpretation makes drawing the attention of the contractual partner,

120 See Chapter 1, part 3.3 of this dissertation.

equivalent to the use of special marks. This approach is widely accepted by judicial practice, regardless of whether it is a B2C contract[121] or a B2B contract.[122]

3.2.3 Slight Differences in Incorporation Control Between B2B and B2C Contracts in Terms of the Explanations

Judicial determinations of drawing attention and of providing an explanation include both a looser approach and a stricter approach.

The difference between the looser approach and the stricter approach is mainly on the burden of proof. The looser approach focuses only on whether the standard business terms with main interests are specially marked, but this approach directly ignores the requirement of an explanation.[123] The looser approach also requires the contractual partner to prove whether he or she had requested the user to explain these standard business terms before the contractual conclusion.[124] After the contractual partner proves this fact, the user will have to prove he or she explained the standard business terms to the contractual partner. In this looser approach, Chinese courts simplify the requirements of drawing attention and providing an explanation to be special marks because it is usually very difficult for the contractual partner to prove his or her request for the explanation.[125] In the stricter approach, once the standard business terms have been specially marked, the burden of proving the completed explanation by the user is directly imposed on the user regardless of whether the contractual partner had asked the user for the above explanation or not, before the contractual conclusion.[126]

It can be found out that Chinese courts tend to adopt the stricter approach more frequently for B2C contracts than for B2B contracts.[127] After all, the judicial

121 Anhui Chi Zhou Intermediate Court 2017 wan 17 minxiazhong 3 (安徽省池州市中级人民法院民事裁定书(2017)皖17民辖终3号).

122 The Supreme Court 2019 minzhong1454 (最高人民法院民事判决书(2019)最高法民终1454号).

123 See the Supreme Court 2017 minshen 4646 (最高人民法院民事裁定书(2017)最高法民申4646号).

124 See the Supreme Court 2018 minshen 1334 (最高人民法院民事裁定书(2018)最高法民申1334号).

125 See Tianjin Second Intermediate Court 2020 jin 02 minzhong 1630 (天津市第二中级人民法院民事判决书(2020)津02民终1630号).

126 See the Supreme Court 2017 qian 03 minzhong 1531 (贵州省遵义市中级人民法院民事判决书(2020)黔03民终1531号).

127 See the Supreme Court 2017 minshen 4646 (最高人民法院民事裁定书(2020)最高法民申2963号).

interpretation of Chinese Contract Law does not refer to the distinction between B2B and B2C contracts.

3.2.4 Jurisdiction Clauses: An Exception

An exception from applying the same treatment of B2B and B2C contracts is set up by another judicial interpretation on the issue of jurisdiction clauses. Art. 31 of the Interpretation on the Application of the Civil Procedure Law of the People's Republic of China (2020 Amendment) states that where an enterprise uses a standard business term against consumers, where there is a choice in this standard business term as to which jurisdiction would apply in the case of potential lawsuits, and where the enterprise does not draw consumers' attention to this standard business term, then the consumers are allowed to claim the standard business term is invalid. In practice though, the Supreme Court has denied the possibility of this interpretation being applied to B2B contracts.[128]

3.3 The Difference in Legal Consequences Between German Law and Chinese Law

Chinese law has additional incorporation control requirements as compared with German law. The German requirements under § 305 II BGB are usually not seen as part of Chinese incorporation control. The German requirements under § 305 II BGB are usually seen as the requirements of contractual conclusion. But this difference over the positioning does not lead to any distinction in legal consequences between Chinese law and German law.

From the perspective of substantial differences in legal consequences between Chinese law and German law, Art. 496 II CCC requires the user to mark a standard business term which concerns a major interest of the contractual partner, and explain it to the contractual partner. These rules apply under Chinese law even if the German requirements under § 305 II BGB are already satisfied by this standard business term. Art. 496 II CCC also means that a standard business term not regarding a major interest of the contractual partner, should also satisfy the German requirements under § 305 II BGB in order to become part of the contract under Chinese law as this standard business term is also subject to the requirements of contractual conclusion.

128 See Beijing Higher Court 2019 minxiazhong 324 (北京市高级人民法院民事裁定书（2019）京民辖终324号).

As a result, Art. 496 II CCC sets additionally higher requirements than those of § 305 II BGB, concerning standard business terms of major interest to the contractual partner. The same requirements as § 305 II BGB are applicable to all standard business terms under Chinese law regardless of whether they concern a main interest of the contractual partner. In the meantime, as in German law, an individually negotiated term is not subject to requirements like those of § 305 II BGB, under Chinese law. As an evaluation by the author, the additional obligations to mark and to explain standard business terms under Art. 497 CCC constitute a more comprehensive protection than § 305 II BGB, which is suitable to the protection of consumers.

In judicial practice, Chinese courts apply both the looser and the stricter interpretations of incorporation control- the former of which is often applied to B2B standard business terms and the latter of which is often applied to B2C standard business terms. For a more suitable legal application or for future legal revisions, German incorporation control, with the requirements of an explicit reminder and the opportunity in an acceptable manner to take note of the content, could be introduced into the Chinese legal practice in order to supplement the drawing attention and explanation requirements under Chinese law as a response to the restriction of the concept of "major interest" concerning the scope of incorporation control.[129]

From the perspective of the differences over legal consequences, B2B standard business terms under Art. 496 II CCC are subject to lower requirements of incorporation control than B2C standard business terms in Chinese judicial practice. That is entirely different from German law. Under German law, B2B standard business terms are directly excluded from the application of incorporation control by § 310 I BGB. In Chinese judicial practice, the user in a B2B transaction still has to mark those standard business terms which concern a major interest of the contractual partner according to Art. 496 II CCC, but the user does not have to explain these terms to the contractual partner.[130] Therefore, it is still far more difficult to incorporate a standard business term into a B2B contract in Chinese law compared with German law. Upon evaluation, the German approach which excludes B2B standard business terms from incorporation control is more appropriate than the Chinese approach of lowering the incorporation control requirements of B2B standard business terms. This is because the incorporation

---

129 See Chapter 4, part 3.2.2.2 of this dissertation.

130 See the Supreme Court, (2019) zuigaofaminzhong 1454 (最高人民法院民事判决书(2019)最高法民终1454号).

control rules are only suitable to the contractual partners with very high needs of protection.

3.4 Summary

After a comparison between German law and Chinese law on incorporation control, we can find great differences between them. Firstly, the object of German incorporation control is all standard business terms while the object of Chinese incorporation control is only the standard business terms concerning major interests of the other party (contractual partner). Secondly, although German incorporation control and Chinese incorporation control aim to give the other party an opportunity to understand standard business terms, the paths adopted by the two countries are different from each other. Chinese incorporation control requires special marks and an active or passive explanation by the user while German incorporation control emphasizes full access to the content of standard business terms and the readability of its content. Thirdly, standard contracts are one of the main objects of Chinese incorporation control but are much less meaningful in German incorporation control. Fourthly, German incorporation control excludes its application to B2B contracts while Chinese legislative regulation does not make the same exclusion.

The most important deficit of Chinese incorporation control is its too-broad scope that includes B2B standard business terms. In Chinese judicial practice, Chinese courts tend to adopt looser approaches for the control of B2B standard business terms than those of B2C standard business terms. However, exceptional cases in judicial practice make this differentiation less clear because there are still some B2B and B2C standard business terms which share similar levels of control. That makes it necessary to discuss clearer methods of differentiating the control of B2B and B2C standard business terms in Chinese law.[131] For this discussion, German incorporation control standards can be a reference.

4 Content Control: § 307 I, II BGB and Art. 497 CCC

The content control rules in the German Civil Code are widely mentioned in Chinese legal studies.[132] Art. 497 CCC has totally different wording but a similar role to that of § 307 BGB. A systematic and detailed understanding of § 307 BGB

---

131 See Chapter 4, part 3.2.2 of this dissertation.

132 For example, QI Chunyi, ZWFX 2013, no. 3, p. 644 ff.; ZHANG Liang, SCDX 2019, no. 1, p. 133 f.

would be helpful in order to introduce the German experience into the interpretation of Art. 497 CCC, understandings and applications of which bring about a lot of disputes.[133]

§ 307 I, II BGB and Art. 497 CCC are as follows:

§ 307 I, II BGB:
"(I) Standard business terms are invalid if, contrary to the requirement of good faith, they unreasonably disadvantage the other party to the contract with the user. An unreasonable disadvantage may also arise from the provision not being clear and comprehensible."
"(II) An unreasonable disadvantage is, in case of doubt, to be assumed to exist if a standard business term
1. is not compatible with essential principles of the statutory provision from which it deviates, or
2. limits main rights or duties inherent in the nature of the contract to such an extent that attainment of the purpose of the contract is jeopardized."
Art. 497 CCC:
"A standard business term is void under any of the following circumstances: (I) existence of a circumstance under which the standard business term is void as provided in Section 3 of Chapter VI of Book One and Article 506 of this Code; (II) the party providing the standard business term unreasonably exempts or alleviates himself from the liability, imposes heavier liability on the other party, or restricts the main rights of the other party; or (III) the party providing the standard clause deprives the other party of his main rights."

4.1 Content Control in § 307 I, II BGB

4.1.1 Unreasonable Disadvantage

According to § 307 I 1 BGB, a standard business term is unreasonable when the user tries to enforce their own interests at the expense of the other party by unilaterally drafting the standard business terms without taking the contractual partner's interests sufficiently into account or granting appropriate compensation for the disadvantages to the contractual partner brought by the standard business terms.[134]

§ 307 I 1 BGB contains two preconditions in content control: a significant disadvantage and reasonableness.[135] To check whether the a standard business term

133 About these disputes see LIANG Huixing, 2014, p. 112.
134 BGHZ 90, 280 (284) = NJW 1984, 1531; BGHZ 120, 108 (118) = NJW 1993, 326; BGH, NJW 1997, 3022; NJW 1999, 2279; NJW 2000, 1110 (1112); BGHZ 120, 118; NJW 2000, 1110; NJW 2003, 887; Jauernig/Stadler BGB § 307 Rn. 5.
135 Cf. UBH/Fuchs § 307 BGB Rn. 98; PWW/Berger BGB § 307 Rn. 7; Stoffels, Rn. 466.

causes an unreasonable disadvantage to the other party, it is necessary to check whether the existence of the standard business terms would put the other party in a more disadvantageous legal position than they would be in in the absence of this term.[136] A slight disadvantage does not constitute a significant disadvantage.[137] In determining whether a disadvantage is unreasonable, it is necessary for the courts to conduct a comprehensive assessment considering the content of the entire contract.[138]

4.1.1.1 The Principle of Equivalence

The determination of the unreasonableness is often expressed as a breach of the principle of equivalence. According to this principle, pre-formulated contractual terms are void if they violate the principle of equivalence between the contractual performance and the consideration against this contractual performance.[139] However, as the question of assessing the reasonableness of the equivalence between the performance and consideration is in principle excluded from content control by Art. 4, Paragraph 2 of Directive 93/13 / EEC and § 307 III 1 BGB, the breach of the principle of equivalence here only includes a fundamental disruption of the balance of contractual rights and obligations,[140] such as a contract term according to which a fitness studio is not available to the contractual partner for several weeks during the holidays of the studio without reducing the price.[141]

4.1.1.2 The Possible Distinction Between B2C and B2B Transactions

In addition to what has already been mentioned, the assessment of the reasonableness of standard business terms should also consider the opinions of the regular participants in this type of transaction.[142] Therefore, the distribution of risks in a standard business term which would be unreasonable as part of a B2C contract, can be valid in a B2B contract. There can be advantages only available to the B2B contractual partners. These advantages will offset the disadvantages arising from the distribution of risks in the standard business term.[143] However,

136 PWW/ Berger BGB § 307 Rn. 7, Staudinger/Wendland BGB § 307 Rn. 89.
137 Wolf/Pfeiffer § 307 BGB Rm. 177; PWW/K.P. Berger § 307 Rn. 7.
138 BGH NJW 2016, 1875 Rn. 43
139 BGHZ 96, 103 (109) = NJW 1986, 179, 180; BGHZ 124, 351 (353) = NJW 1994, 1060 (1061); BGH NJW 2001, 2635 (2637).
140 Cf. MüKoBGB/Wurmnest BGB § 307 Rn. 54.
141 LG Frankenthal VuR 1993, 350 (351).
142 MüKoBGB/Wurmnest § 307 Rn. 40.
143 Cf. BT-Drs. 7/3919, 23; MüKoBGB/Wurmnest BGB § 307 Rn. 40.

it is still to be answered how to find out the above-mentioned "opinions of the regular participants" in a specific type of transaction.[144]

4.1.1.3 *Summation Effect and Compensation Effect*

According to German case law, contractual terms lead to the validity of a standard business term if the standard business term is harmless in itself, but, the overall effect together with other terms in the same contract, leads to an unreasonable disadvantage for the other party.[145]

This is usually called a "summation effect." Such a summation effect can also result from the interaction of individually negotiated terms and standard business terms.[146] The summation effect refers to the judicial evaluation going beyond a single standard business term- creating an opportunity for the test of reasonableness to apply to the entire content of the contract.[147]

The perspective of the compensation effect is similar to that of the summation effect. Also from the entire content of the contract, a disadvantageous standard business term can be compensated by advantages granted to the other party through another standard business term or individually negotiated term[148] if the advantages and disadvantages are so factually connected and can be viewed as an overall regulation of the same topic.[149] The advantages must however compensate for the disadvantages appropriately.[150]

4.1.2 *Deviation from Default Rules*

According to § 307 II Nr. 1 BGB, a deviation from the essential basic ideas of default rules would be an indication of an unreasonable disadvantage within the meaning of § 307 I BGB.[151] That means that default rules provide more concrete criteria for content control than the rules of unreasonable disadvantage in § 307 I BGB. This interpretation of § 307 II Nr. 1 BGB was introduced by scholars into Chinese academic discussions a long time ago and can help to make Art. 497

---

144 See Chapter 4 of this dissertation.
145 UBH/Ulmer § 307 BGB Rn. 155.
146 BGH NJW 2006, 2116 (2117).
147 Cf. BGH NJW 2006, 2116 (2117); Staudinger/Wendland § 307, Rn. 139; BeckOGK/Eckelt § 307, Rn. 85; Klimke, JR 2007, 353.; MüKoBGB/Wurmnest BGB § 307 Rn. 37.
148 MüKoBGB/Wendland BGB § 307 Rn. 38.
149 BGH NJW 2003, 888 (889 f.).
150 Staudinger/Wendland BGB § 307 Rn. 125; Bamberger/Roth/H. Schmit BGB § 307 Rn. 21; Stoffels Rn. 487.
151 BGH v. 04.11.1992—VIII ZR 235/91—juris Rn. 26—BGHZ 120, 108.

CCC concrete in its applications. Therefore, it is necessary to understand the application of default rules in the context of content control under § 307 II Nr. 1 BGB.

4.1.2.1 The Model Function of Default Rules

The German case law attaches default rules to a model function (Leitbildfunktion) in content control, and thus default rules here become to some degree "mandatory."[152] That means it is possible to invalidate standard business terms just because they breach important default rules significantly. This role of default rules derives from their function to complement the loopholes of juridical acts in the theory of civil law that is well-known in civil law countries.[153] Default rules, as the models for content control, do not include those based on expediency considerations but rather only those which express the idea of justice.[154] An example is that a standard business term prescribing that a broker will get a commission regardless of brokerage success and therefore deviating from § 652 BGB, should be void.[155]

4.1.2.2 Controversial Understandings of the Legal Rules in § 307 II Nr. 1 BGB

In the academic opinions and judicial practice of Germany, there are different understandings of the "legal rules" in § 307 II Nr. 1 BGB, although all of these opinions recognize the statutory default rules as being part of the "legal rules" § 307 II Nr. 1 BGB and their model function. Among them, the narrowest interpretation of "legal rules" includes only the statutory default rules. In other words, only the default rules in legislation and ordinances shaping the private law are legal rules in § 307 II Nr. 1 BGB. Accordingly, general legal principles, analogous application of the statutory default rules, or other rules developed by case law do not constitute "legal rules" according to the meaning of § 307 II Nr. 1 BGB based on the narrowest interpretation.[156]

On the contrary, the broadest interpretation of "legal rules" includes all general legal principles abstracted from the legal system. That means, in addition to the statutory default rules, that all legal principles derived from case law or

152 Palandt/Heinrichs § 307 BGB Rn. 25.
153 See Chapter 4, part 3.1 of this dissertation.
154 BGH NJW 2007, 3637 Rn 22c; cf. BGHZ 89, 206; BGH NJW 1991, 1886; 1991, 2414; NJW-RR 1996, 1009; NJW 1997, 1700; 2001, 3480.
155 BGHZ 99, 374; BGH NJW 2010, 3568; OLG Oldenburg MDR 2005, 1287.
156 Cf. Graba in: Schlosser/Coester-Waltjen/Graba, AGBG § 9 Rn. 26.

legal doctrines, analogous application of the statutory default rules, and judicial developments of law, belong to the "legal rules" of § 307 II Nr. 1 BGB.[157]

The third interpretation tries to find a balance between the above two opinions. According to the third interpretation, statutory and non-statutory default rules and their analogous applications should be considered to constitute the "legal rules" of § 307 II Nr. 1 BGB under the premise that their content is concrete enough to be compared with a standard business term and for it to be determined whether they deviate from the default rules.[158]

In addition to the above opinions, some German courts also apply mandatory rules as the "legal rules" in § 307 II Nr. 1 BGB to invalidate standard business terms,[159] which makes the understanding of "legal rules" in § 307 II Nr. 1 BGB more complicated.

Based on the mission of § 307 II Nr. 1 BGB set by the legislator, the understanding of "legal rules" in § 307 II Nr. 1 BGB needs to meet the following precondition: a legal rule should precisely regulate the objective that is also regulated by the standard business term to be examined.[160] To satisfy this criteria, a legal rule within the meaning of § 307 II Nr. 1 BGB must have unambiguous content.

General legal principles are inconsistent with this mission of § 307 II Nr. 1 BGB. General legal principles are too abstract and do not specify facts to be regulated and legal consequences for the comparison between "legal rules" and standard business terms in content control.[161] Therefore, the "legal rules" within the meaning of § 307 II Nr. 1 BGB should be limited to those legal rules with clear content,[162] no matter whether they are statutory or non-statutory.

As for mandatory legal rules, although they are valuations of the legislator, it is not suitable to consider them as part of the legal rules within the meaning of § 307 II Nr. 1 BGB. This is because standard business terms in violation of mandatory rules are directly void, and there is no need to test their reasonableness based on § 307 BGB.[163] Content control is a stricter restriction on the validity of standard business terms than mandatory rules. German courts are increasingly inclined to apply mandatory rules in content control under § 307 Abs 2 Nr 1 BGB in order to expand the scope of § 1 UKlaG to include standard business

157 NK-BGB/Knollmann, § 307 Rn. 29.
158 Cf. Becker, S. 87.
159 BGH NJW 1983, 1320 (1322); OLG Düsseldorf BB 1981, 1663.
160 BGH NJW 1980, 1625 (1626).
161 Cf. Becker, S. 87.
162 Cf. Becker, S. 87.
163 UBH /Fuchs § 307 BGB Rn 208; Staudinger/Wendland § 307 BGB Rn. 19.

terms in the violation of mandatory rules into representative legal actions (Ver bandsklageverfahren).[164] However, this is more appropriate through the teleological interpretation of § 1 UKlaG, rather than through blurring the boundary between content control and the application of mandatory rules.[165]

An exception is that German courts can declare a standard business term's invalidity based on §§ 307 ff. BGB for the reason of procedure economy (Prozessökonomie) where there are doubts about whether a rule breached by this standard business term is mandatory or not.[166]

In summary, the legal rules within the meaning of § 307 II Nr. 1 BGB could be both statutory and non-statutory default rules and their analogous applications, under the premise that they have clear content expressing the idea of justice. General legal principles and mandatory rules should not be included as part of legal rules.

The model function of the default rules is based on its complementary function to loopholes of juridical acts. The complementary function means default rules are considered as part of a contract on the issues where both parties to the contract have not reach any agreement after negotiations. In this complementary function, default rules are considered reasonable for both parties to the contract. In content control process, default rules set models to show how reasonable standard business terms should be. The model function of the default rules could also be useful in content control process of other countries, where the dichotomy between default and mandatory rule is also recognized, for example, China.[167]

4.1.3 Jeopardizing the Contractual Purpose

4.1.3.1 The Role of § 307 II Nr. 2 in Relation to Nr. 1

A standard business term that is incompatible with essential ideas of legal rules can also jeopardize the purpose of the contract.[168] For example, an invalid standard business term in a rental contract, according to which the landlord renting out his restaurant bears no liability for the business license, is subject to both § 307 II Nr. 1 and Nr. 2 BGB.[169] Therefore, there are opinions that the scopes of application of § 307 II Nr. 1 and Nr. 2 BGB partially overlap.[170]

---

164 Staudinger/Wendland § 307 BGB Rn. 20.
165 Id.
166 Staudinger/Wendland § 307 BGB Rn. 19.
167 See Chapter 5, part 5 of this dissertation.
168 UBH/Fuchs § 307 BGB Rn. 197.
169 UBH/Fuchs § 307 BGB Rn. 197.
170 Wolf/Pfeiffer § 307 BGB Rn. 97; UBH/Fuchs § 307 BGB Rn. 197.

However, it should also be recognized that § 307 II Nr. 2 BGB plays a major role where there is a lack of legal rules according to the meaning of § 307 II Nr. 1 BGB.[171] Otherwise, it would not be necessary to add Nr. 2 into § 307 II BGB. The differentiation between § 307 II Nr 1 and Nr. 2 BGB could also be that the courts should apply an existing "legal rule" to compare with the standard business term in question or develop a judicial rule based on their understanding of the purpose of the contract in question.

4.1.3.2 The Constituent Elements of § 307 II Nr. 2 BGB and the Relationship Between Them

The constituent elements and their connections with each other are prescribed clearly in § 307 II Nr. 2 BGB. According to its wording, "the major rights and obligations" derive from the "nature of the contract," and the fundamental criteria concerns whether the restriction of the major rights and obligations jeopardizes "the purpose of the contract."

In theory, "the nature of the contract" is primarily shaped by the type of contract, its economic purpose, and other typical objectives.[172] The purpose of the contract is the economic goals and ideas of the contractual partner.[173] According to these understandings, the major rights and obligations are fundamental and formative for establishing the type of contract.[174] However, none of the above explanations are of great meaning in practice.

What is clear is a judicial rule developed by courts to be compared with the content of the standard business term in content control has to be derived from the objectified goals of the contract in the application of § 307 II Nr. 2 BGB.[175] And § 307 II Nr. 2 BGB is particularly set for unregulated types of contracts by law.[176]

In other words, § 307 II Nr. 2 BGB is a tool for developing new judicial rules from an objective respective. These new judicial rules are comprised of major rights and obligations from which standard business terms are not allowed to deviate. This tool requires the courts to interpret the objective purpose of the contract and forbids standard business terms from jeopardizing this purpose of

171 Jauernig/Stadler BGB § 307 Rn. 12; Erman/Roloff/Looschelders BGB § 307 Rn. 31.
172 Erman/Roloff/Looschelders BGB § 307 Rn. 31.
173 Erman/Roloff/Looschelders BGB § 307 Rn. 34.
174 Staudinger/Wendland BGB § 307 Rn. 272.
175 Cf. Oechsler, S. 320 f.
176 UBH/Fuchs § 307 BGB Rn. 97.

the contract. § 307 II Nr. 2 BGB thus could be summarized as jeopardizing the purpose of the contract.[177] There is practically no need to differentiate between the purpose of the contract, the nature of the contract, and the major rights and obligations.[178] The core mission of § 307 II Nr. 2 BGB is to find out what rights or obligations are major based on the objective goals of the contract.

4.1.3.3 The Cardinal Obligations

§ 307 II Nr. 2 is also linked to the German case law, according to which the user is not allowed to release themself from the non-fulfillment of "cardinal obligations" or to significantly reduce their liabilities originating from this non-fulfillment.[179] In other words, the protection of cardinal obligations is to be understood in a broad sense, as including the prohibition of an exemption or alleviation from both the cardinal obligations and liabilities.

The major rights and obligations within the contract are the prerequisites for the fulfillment of the contract and are indispensable for achieving the purpose of the contract.[180] The major rights and obligations here are a repeated expression as the major rights of the contractual partner are the major obligations of the user. Thus, the meaning of the major rights and obligations within the contract (§ 307 II Nr. 2 BGB) is the same as that of the cardinal obligations of the user in the case law. This understanding of rights and obligations is useful for interpreting Art. 497 CCC, where rights and liabilities are also referred to.[181]

Cardinal obligations are the obligations that are not allowed to be restricted, on which the proper execution of the contract depends, and fulfillment of which the contractual partner legitimately expects.[182] Cardinal obligations include the main performance obligations (Hauptleistungspflichten),[183] which form the basis of the existence of the contract.[184] The main performance obligations (if

177 Guhling/Günter/Guhling, BGB § 307 Rn. 48 f.
178 Cf. Staudinger/Wendland BGB § 307 Rn. 272.
179 BGHZ 49, 363; 50, 20; 72, 208; NJW-RR 2005, 1496 (1505); NJW-RR 2004, 900.
180 BGH NJW 1985, 3016; 1993, 335.
181 See Chapter 5, part 5.1.1 of this dissertation.
182 BGHZ 149, 60, 89; BGHZ 145, 203; TranspR 2002, 448; Jauernig/Stadler BGB § 307 Rn. 12.
183 Cf. BGH NJW 1968, 1567; NJW 1985, 3016; NJW-RR 2000, 998; NJW 2002, 673; WM 2005, 656; NJW 2005, 1774.
184 Cf. Looschelders, S. 3 f.

they are controllable according to § 307 III 1 BGB) belong almost always to the major rights and obligations in § 307 II Nr. 2 BGB.[185]

In order to judge whether a standard business term restricting or excluding ancillary performance obligations endangers the purpose of the contract, ancillary performance obligations (Nebenleistungspflichten) must be carefully checked in terms of their weight for the contractual interests of the contractual partner. The answer is yes if the ancillary performance obligations restricted or excluded by the standard business term are closely related to the main performance obligations. For example, in insurance contracts, the purpose of the contract is only endangered if the contract becomes futile due to the improper conception of insured risks.[186]

According to German case law, cardinal obligations also include the obligations of care (Sorgfaltspflichten), which are intended to protect the contractual partner from damages that the user should typically bear without standard business terms.[187] For example, the entrepreneur of a car-washing shop has the cardinal obligation to protect the vehicles from damage during the washing process.[188]

4.2 Content Control in Art. 497 CCC

4.2.1 Three Legal Articles but Only One Usual Legal Basis

Art. 26 II, III of CRIPL: "Business operators shall not, by standard business terms and conditions, notices, declarations, on-site posters, and other means, impose unfair or unreasonable rules on consumers to exclude or restrict consumer rights, reduce or waive the liabilities of business operators, or aggravate the liabilities of consumers, among others, and shall not force consumers into any transactions by standard terms and conditions and technical means. If the standard business terms, notices, declarations, and on-site posters, among others, contain any rules as mentioned in the preceding paragraph, such rules shall be void."

Article 19 of Insurance Law IL: "The following clauses in an insurance contract concluded with the standard business terms provided by the insurer are invalid: (1) exempting the insurer from legal liabilities or increasing the liabilities

185 Cf. BGH NJW 2002, 673 (675); NJW 2005, 1774; OLG Saarbrücken NJW-RR 1995, 117 (118); Palandt / Grüneberg BGB § 307 Rn 33; Staudinger/Wendland BGB § 307 Rn. 273.

186 BGH BeckRS 2017, 119229 Rn. 15.

187 Erman/Roloff/Looschelders BGB § 307 Rn. 33.

188 BGH NJW 2005, 422; KG NJW-RR 1991, 698.

of the applicant or the insured; (2) excluding the rights enjoyed by the policyholder, the insured or the beneficiary according to law."

Chinese law contains three articles concerning content control: Art. 497 CCC, Art. 26 CRIPL and Art. 19 IL (Insurance Law). These three legal articles enumerate invalid terms with two concepts: liabilities and rights. Although there are indeed differences between the above three articles, for example, Art. 26 CRIPL uses consumer rights instead of the main rights in Art. 497 CCC and the subjects of the rights in Art. 19 IL includes the insured and the beneficiary who is possibly not the other party to the contract, the main legal basis in the Chinese judicial content control is usually Art. 497 CCC (formerly Art. 40 CCL). Chinese courts usually pay no attention to the difference in the wordings when applying them to B2C contracts or B2B contracts.[189]

Art. 497 CCC consists of three points. Among them, No. 2 and 3 are adopted specially for content control of standard business terms. No. 1 only reminds the courts of mandatory rules that can also be applied to invalidate contractual terms.

Because of the vague wording of Art. 497 CCC, Art. 26 CRIPL and Art. 19 IL and the very minimal difference between them, it makes no difference which article is used as the legal basis for content control. The usual legal basis in the legal practice is Art. 497 (or formerly Art. 40 CCL).[190]

4.2.2 *Normative Positioning*

Art. 497 CCC does not mention the principle of good faith or other legal principles. There are no more concrete legal provisions in the Chinese Civil Code or CRIPL for content control such as legal provisions like §§ 308, 309 BGB. There are different opinions in Chinese literature on the positioning of Art. 497 CCC. Since the discussion of the control of standard business terms in Chinese civil law is often carried out with reference to German civil law, the positioning of Art. 497 CCC is also based on its comparison with §§ 307 ff. BGB. In the older

189 See Changzhou Intermediate Court (2020) su 04 minzhong 577 (江苏省常州市中级人民法院(2020)苏 04 民终577 号民事判决书); Foshan Intermediate Court (2018) yue06minzhong4014 (广东省佛山市中级人民法院 (2018)粤 06 民终 4014 号判决书).

190 For example, Zhumadian Intermediate Court (2017) yu 17 minzhong 1122 (河南省驻马店市中级人民法院(2017)豫17民终1122号民事判决书); Beijing Haidian District Court (2005) haiminchuzi 23337 (北京市海淀区人民法院（2005）海民初字第23337号).

opinion, it was thought that Art. 497 CCC is a blacklist similar to § 309 BGB,[191] which contains prohibitions without spaces of judicial evaluation. However, the newer view is that Art. 497 CCC is purely a general clause similar to § 307 I BGB.[192]

By analyzing the content of Art. 497 CCC, it is not difficult to find that Art. 497 is not as concrete as §§ 308, 309 BGB, which contain lists of specific examples of invalid standard business terms with respective scopes of application, but it is obvious that Art. 497 CCC is also not as abstract as § 307 I BGB. Although the content of Art. 497 CCC is still relatively abstract compared with §§ 308, 309 BGB, it is not a statement of general legal principles. Art. 497 CCC lists the circumstances of invalid standard business terms, and these circumstances are far more concrete than the unreasonable disadvantages or a breach of good faith in § 307 I BGB. Therefore, the level of concreteness of Art. 497 CCC lies somewhere between § 307 I BGB and §§ 308, 309 BGB. § 307 II BGB is a typical legal standard (typische rechtliche Kriterien) as it is a preliminary concretization of § 307 I BGB[193] and is much more concrete than §§ 308, 309 BGB. Based on the above comparison, we can see that the positioning and function of Art. 497 CCC is analogous to § 307 II BGB, which can also be proved by the views of Chinese legislators.[194]

4.2.3 Judicial Arguments in the Relevant Practice

In judicial practice, Chinese courts, in fact, rarely check standard business terms concretely based on how the standard business terms exempt or alleviate the user from specific liabilities, how they impose specific heavier liabilities on the other party, or how they restrict the main rights of the other party. Instead, the approach of judicial practice bypasses the concrete content of Art. 497 CCC. Art. 497 CCC has become the legal basis for declaring that the Chinese courts have the power to invalidate standard business terms instead of relying on the legal criterion of content control.[195] That means, although Chinese courts usually

---

191 See Gao Shengping, HNSD p. 73.

192 See He Xuxu, SZDX p. 58.

193 Cf. Palandt/Grüneberg BGB § 307 Rn. 28.

194 See HUANG Wei, p. 956.

195 See Meizhou Intermediate Court (2021) yue 14 minzhong 886 (广东省梅州市中级人民法院 (2021)粤 14 民终 886 号民事判决书)； Lasa Intermediate Court (2021) zang 01 minzhong 800 (西藏自治区拉萨市中级人民法院 (2021)藏 01 民终 800 号民事判决书).

declare the legal basis of judicial content control is Art. 497 No. 2 or No. 3 CCC, the arguments that they use to demonstrate whether the standard business terms are valid is not Art. 497 CCC itself.

Research conducted by the author shows that the real criteria introduced into judicial rulings to demonstrate the validity or invalidity of standard business terms are as follows:

(a) General legal principles, such as the principle of fairness[196] and good faith.[197] Although Art. 497 CCC does not mention general legal principles like § 307 I 1 BGB, an important argument used to invalidate standard business terms is a breach of the principle of fairness or good faith. For example, a standard business term excluding refunds under any condition written into a contract for English classes is void because it breaches the principle of fairness.[198]

(b) Factors related to transactions, including the purpose of the contract,[199] the unilateral superiority of the user,[200] and the reasonable distribution of risks.[201] An example of the user's unilateral superiority is that the user as an insurer imposes its standard business terms on the contractual partner.[202] The reasonable distribution of risks means that the distribution of risks in a

196 See Beijing Second Intermediate Court (2021) jing 02 minzhong 10057 (北京市第二中级人民法院(2021)京02民终10057号民事判决书)； the Supreme Court 2005 No. 4 (顾骏诉上海交行储蓄合同纠纷案，《最高人民法院公报》 2005年第4期).

197 See Hubei Yicang Intermediate Court (2015) eyichangzhongminyi 00767 (湖北省宜昌市中级人民法院(2015)鄂宜昌中民一终字第00767号判决书)； Jiangsu Taizhou Intermediate Court(2020) su12minzhong1272(江苏省泰州市中级人民法院(2020)苏12民终1272号民事判决书)； Jiangsu Yancheng Intermediate Court (2020) su 09 minzhong 4536(江苏省盐城市中级人民法院(2020)苏09民终4536号民事判决书).

198 Jiangsu Higher Court 2018 No. 6 p. 23–26 (《江苏省高级人民法院公报》 2018年第6辑总第60辑第23–26页).

199 See Shanghai Higher Court (2018) huminzhong 81 (上海市高级人民法院（2018）沪民终81号判决书) ； the Supreme Court (2018) minzai 275 (最高人民法院(2018)最高法民再275号判决书).

200 See Jiangsu Changzhou(2020) su 04 minzhong 577 (江苏省常州市中级人民法院(2020)苏04民终577号民事判决书) ； Guangdong Foshan Intermediate Court 2018 yue 06 mizhong 4014 (广东省佛山市中级人民法院(2018)粤06民终4014号判决书).

201 Guangdong Higher Court (2016) yueminzhong 1551 (广东省高级人民法院(2016)粤民终1551号判决书).

202 Jiangsu Changzhou Intermediate Court (2020) su 04 minzhong 577 (江苏省常州市中级人民法院民事判决书(2020)苏04民终577号).

standard business term is normal, and the contractual partner has an opportunity to purchase insurance to avoid these risks.[203]
A breach of the purpose of the contract is also an argument made during content control checks. Sometimes a breach of the purpose of the contract is connected to a breach of the principle of fairness or is considered to be the reason why the principle of fairness is breached.[204]

(c) other legal rules, including statutory legal rules[205] and judicial interpretations of the Supreme Court.[206]

4.3 Summary

The Chinese regulation on content control is totally different from the German regulation if we only focus on their wording. However, the default rules and the contractual purpose can be found not only in German law but also in Chinese legal practice concerning content control. Among Art. 497 CCC, Art. 26 CRIPL and Art. 19 IL, the usual legal basis in legal practice for content control is Art. 497 CCC. The positioning and function of Art. 497 CCC is analogous to § 307 II BGB. In the meantime, the Chinese regulation, Art. 497 CCC, brings a lot of clarity to the difficulties with it. Chinese legal practice deviates from Art. 497 CCC to some degree. Art. 497 CCC requires an interpretation connected to the practice. The German experience on the applications of the default rules and the contractual purpose in content control is able to provide help with this.

What should not be ignored is that both the Chinese content control rules and the German content control rules require a differentiation between B2C and B2B

203 Kunming Railway Intermediate Court (2016) yun 71 minzhong 10 (昆明铁路运输中级法院(2016)云71民终10号判决书).

204 Chinalawinfo CLI.C.84175722 (杭州互联网法院成立两周年十大影响力案件之六：陈某诉杭州某软件服务有限公司网络服务合同纠纷案——流量劫持、用户Cookie记录隐私与证据开示的司法认定；【法宝引证码】：CLI.C.84175722).

205 See Jilin Changchun Intermediate Court (2015) changminsizhong 487 (吉林省长春市中级人民法院(2015)长民四终字第487号民事判决书)； Jiangsu Nanjing Intermediate Court (2019) su 01 minzhong 8112 (江苏省南京市中级人民法院(2019)苏 01 民终 8112 号民事判决书); The Supreme Court 2020, no. 1, pp. 44–46 (刘智超诉同方知网(北京)技术有限公司买卖合同纠纷案，《最高人民法院公报》2020年第1期，第44–46页).

206 See Shanghai First Intermediate Court (2010) huyizhongminliushangchu 22 (上海市第一中级人民法院（2010）沪一中民六(商)初字第22号判决书).

contracts. That also makes this differentiation the common problem faced by the Chinese law and the German law.[207]

5 Other Regulations on the Control of Standard Business Terms

The emphasis of the above comparison between Chinese law and German law focuses on §§ 305, 307 I, II BGB and Art. 496-497 CCC. But other regulations on the control of standard business terms are also worth mentioning in order to draw a complete comparison between the two countries.

5.1 §§ 305a-306a BGB and Art. 498 CCC

§ 305a BGB sets up exceptions to the incorporation control rules under § 305 II BGB. The reason for these exceptions is that government organs are involved in the creation of the standard business terms listed in § 305a BGB and they guarantee a certain degree of publicity so that the reference is unnecessary in individual cases and the possibility of knowledge exists.[208] In the Chinese Civil Code, there are no such exceptions for the control of standard business terms.

§ 305b BGB prescribes that individually negotiated terms take precedence of the application over standard business terms. A similar regulation of the Chinese Civil Code is Art. 498 S. 3 CCC. According to Art. 498 S. 3 CCC, "the non-standard contractual term shall prevail where its content is inconsistent with that of a standard business term."

§ 305c I BGB excludes surprising terms from being incorporated into contracts. Although there are many discussions on surprising terms in Chinese academic literature, there is no such counterpart in the Chinese Civil Code. On the other hand, § 305c II BGB does have a counterpart in the Chinese Civil Code. According to § 305c II BGB, the interpretation of a standard business term should be against the user where there are ambiguities in its wording. According to Art. 498 S. 1 and S. 2 CCC, a standard business term should be interpreted in accordance with its common understanding where there is a dispute over the understanding of a standard business term. The standard business term shall also be interpreted against the user where there can be two or more interpretations of a standard business term. That means the German Civil Code and the Chinese Civil Code are the same on the interpretation of standard business terms.

207 See Chapters 2 and 4 of this dissertation.
208 MüKoBGB/Basedow BGB § 305a Rn. 1.

§ 306 BGB regulates the legal consequences of the invalidity or non-incorporation of standard business terms, according to which the validity of the rest of the contract should be maintained, and any loopholes in the contract are to be filled by the superseded default rules. In addition, § 306a BGB contains a prohibition on circumvention. Both § 306 BGB and § 306a BGB are widely recognized as an unwritten rule in Chinese law.

5.2 §§ 307 ff. BGB

5.2.1 The Transparency Requirement

The transparency requirement obliges the user to formulate the rights and obligations of the contractual partner as clearly as possible and to present them transparently.[209] The standard business terms, in which the contract's subject matter is described, are excluded from content control according to § 307 III 1 BGB but these terms are also subject to a requirement of transparency according to § 307 III 2 BGB.

Under the requirement of transparency, the user should make their standard business terms linguistically understandable. The user should also describe the economic disadvantages clearly and burdens of the contractual partner resulting from the standard business terms[210] and all the consequences foreseeable for the average contractual partner with the considerations of the circumstances.[211] As a result, the contractual partner should identify his rights and obligations with no need for help or advice.[212] There is no regulation for the above requirement of transparency in the Chinese Civil Code. The Chinese courts often use transparency as an argument to determine a contractual term as being an individually negotiated term.[213]

5.2.2 §§ 308, 309 BGB and the Interpretation of Art. 497 CCC

The prohibitions in § 308 BGB are the standard business terms that often or typically violate § 307 BGB. These prohibitions are listed with indefinite concepts

209 BeckOGK/Schmidt BGB § 307 Rn. 45; cf. Wolf/Pfeiffer Rn. 234.

210 BGH NJW-RR 2020, 112 Rn. 23; v. Westphalen NJW 2020, 280 (282).

211 BGH NJW-RR 2020, 112 Rn. 23; NZG 2019, 703 Rn. 12; NJW 2018, 1811 Rn. 11; 2018, 1544 Rn. 8; WM 2017, 517 Rn. 15; NJW 2016, 1575 Rn. 31; BeckOGK /Schmidt BGB § 307 Rn. 45.

212 BGH NJW-RR 2020, 112 Rn. 23; BeckOGK /Schmidt BGB § 307 Rn. 45.

213 For example, the Supreme Court (2015) minshen 137 (最高人民法院民事裁定书(2015)民申字第137号).

such as "unreasonable," "reasonable," "without an objectively justified reason," and definite descriptions. The prohibitions in § 308 BGB summarize those standard business terms which in practice often lead to an unreasonable disadvantage for the contractual partner. At the same time, § 308 BGB leaves spaces for judicial valuations.

In contrast to § 308 BGB, the spaces in § 309 BGB for judicial evaluation are narrower. In principle, the prohibitions of § 309 BGB differ from those of § 308 BGB.

§ 309 BGB does not contain any indefinite concepts and leaves no space for judicial evaluation. However, it does not mean that there is definitely no space for legal interpretation. For example, "material" in Nr. 5 lit. b, "disproportionate" in Nr. 8 lit. b dd and "much higher" in Nr. 15 lit. a all need judicial interpretation.

There are connections between § § 308, 309 and § 307 BGB. § 307 BGB seeks to cover the wide range of unreasonable standard business terms with the help of abstract criteria. In contrast, § 309 BGB describes a smaller core area, in which precisely defined standard business terms are invalid.

There is no counterpart to § § 308, 309 BGB in Chinese law. That is the reason why Art. 497 CCC is more important for content control in China. The interpretation of Art. 497 CCC, therefore, needs to provide criteria for content control.[214]

5.2.3 *The Roles of §§ 308, 309 BGB in the Future Legislative Revisions of the Chinese Civil Code*

Although §§ 308, 309 BGB do not have counterparts in the Chinese Civil Code, most of the prohibitions in §§ 308, 309 BGB can be references for future revisions of the Chinese Civil Code because they give more concrete instructions to content control. There are already prohibitions in § 309 BGB covered by general legal regulations on contracts in the Chinese Civil Code; therefore, there is no need to add these prohibitions into future legislative revisions. This dissertation is not able to analyze every prohibition in §§ 308, 309 BGB. It will instead discuss some examples of them.

An example from § 308 BGB that can be a reference for future Chinese legislative changes is § 308 Nr. 3 BGB. § 308 Nr. 3 BGB (reservation of the right to revoke) declares that a standard business term is invalid, where the content states, "the agreement on a right of the user to free himself from his obligation to perform without any objectively justified reason indicated in the contract" (this does not apply to continuing obligations). This regulation restricts the free

214 Cf. MüKo/Wurmnest § 309 Rn. 4.

autonomy of rights of withdrawal granted by § 346 I BGB.[215] This prohibition is very different from the Chinese regulation that only focuses on ascertaining the contractual freedom to set up a reservation of either side's right to revoke a contract under Art. 562 II CCC.

Because the Chinese law does not give definite restrictions on the reservation of the user's right to revoke the contract, Chinese courts have to interpret Art. 497 II CCC if they want to set similar restrictions. This approach brings legal uncertainty. The introduction of a similar regulation to § 308 Nr. 3 BGB into the Chinese Civil Code is, therefore, necessary for future Chinese legislative changes.

Another example in § 309 BGB that can be a reference for future Chinese legislative changes is § 309 Nr. 6 BGB. § 309 Nr. 6 BGB (contractual penalty) is "a provision by which the user is promised the payment of a contractual penalty in the event of non-acceptance or late acceptance of the performance, payment default or in the event that the other party to the contract frees himself from the contract" should be invalid.

§ 309 Nr. 6 BGB is based on the legislative assessment that the user can also insert a standard business term of lump-sum damages granting themself protection against the breaches of duty listed but under the premise that not too much burden is to be placed on the other side of the user.[216]

Although Art. 585[217] II CCC allows Chinese courts to adjust the amount of lump-sum damages when it is excessively higher than the loss caused, a supplementary regulation like § 309 Nr. 6 BGB would restrict the use of standard business terms over lump-sum damages further protecting the contractual partner from the user. Therefore, it is also worthwhile to consider adding a

---

215 Wolf/Lindacher/Pfeiffer/Dammann § 308 Nr. 3 Rn. 1; BGH NJW 2008, 360 Rn. 40.

216 MüKoBGB/Wurmnest § 309 Nr. 7 Rn. 2; Grüneberg/Grüneberg § 309 Nr. 7 Rn. 33.

217 Art. 585 CCC: "The parties may agree that, upon default by a party, a certain amount of liquidated damages shall be paid to the other party according to the circumstance of the breach, or the parties may agree on the method of calculating the compensation for losses arising from the breach.
Where the agreed liquidated damages are lower than the loss caused, the people's court or an arbitration institution may increase the amount upon request of a party. Where the agreed liquidated damages are excessively higher than the loss caused, the people's court or an arbitration institution may make an appropriate reduction upon request of a party.
Where the parties agree on the liquidated damages for delayed performance, the breaching party shall continue to perform the obligation after paying the liquidated damages."

regulation like § 309 Nr. 6 BGB in future legislative changes of the Chinese Civil Code.

§ 309 Nr. 7 BGB is the only prohibitions in §§ 308, 309 BGB with no need to be added in the future Chinese legislative revisions.

The prohibitions in § 309 Nr. 7 Exclusion of liability for injury to life, body or health and in case of gross fault are: a) Injury to life, body or health- any exclusion or limitation of liability for damage from injury to life, body or health due to negligent breach of obligation by the user or intentional or negligent breach of duty by a legal representative or a person used to perform an obligation of the user; and b) Gross fault- any exclusion or limitation of liability for other damage arising from a grossly negligent breach of obligation by the user or from an intentional or grossly negligent breach of duty by a legal representative of the user or a person used to perform an obligation of the user.

A very similar regulation in the Chinese Civil Code to § 309 Nr. 7 BGB is Art. 506 CCC. The content of Art. 506 CCC is "an exculpatory clause in a contract exempting liability on the following acts is void: (1) causing physical injury to the other party; or (2) causing losses to the other party's property intentionally or due to gross negligence."

A comparison between Art. 506 CCC and § 309 Nr. 7 BGB shows that the prohibited content of contractual terms is almost the same. The difference is that Art. 506 CCC is applicable not only to standard business terms but also to individually negotiated terms, while § 309 Nr. 7 BGB is only applicable to standard business terms.

It is another question whether the scope of Art. 506 CCC is too large as it includes individually negotiated terms. As for the control of standard business terms, there is no need to add a new regulation like § 309 Nr. 7 BGB. The future legislative changes of the Chinese Civil Code may consider whether the scope of Art. 506 CCC should be restricted only to standard business terms like § 309 Nr. 7 BGB.

5.3 Summary

Except for § 305c II BGB, there is no counterpart to §§ 305a-306a BGB in the Chinese Civil Code. Among §§ 307 ff. BGB, the requirement of transparency under § 307 III BGB and §§ 308, 309 BGB have no counterpart in the Chinese Civil Code either. Most of the prohibitions in §§ 308, 309 BGB can be references for future Chinese legislative changes to add more concrete criteria for content control. The exception is § 309 Nr. 7 BGB because its scope and content are already covered by Art. 506 CCC.

6 The Relationship Between Incorporation Control and Content Control

Although the boundary between the incorporation control and the content control rules is theoretically clear, it is sometimes not easy to differentiate between them in practice. Where the content of standard business terms is unacceptable, the Chinese courts often declare that the user has not drawn the attention of the contractual partner to these terms or not explained them to the contractual partner.[218] The Chinese courts often avoid checking the reasonableness of these standard business terms directly. The German courts do not always abide by the boundary between incorporation control and content control either.

6.1 The German Law

6.1.1 Procedural Economic Reasons

It is strictly only possible to carry out the content control assessment of a standard business term if this term is already incorporated into a contract.[219] The incorporation control assessment does not aim to check the reasonableness of the content of standard business terms. Nevertheless, legal consequences of both types of control are identical, and the strictness of content control and the strictness of incorporation control are complementary. Therefore, it is also acceptable if the judicial practice for procedural economic reasons commits incorporation control of a standard business term flexibly because this term is anyway to be qualified as invalid.[220] And strict incorporation control is usually followed by loose content control or vice versa.[221]

The above combination between incorporation control and content control avoids unnecessary, double-thorough judicial checks. Thus, it is based on procedural economic reasons.

---

218 Shanhai First Intermediate Court (2020) hu 01 minzhong10251(上海市第一中级人民法院(2020)沪01民终10251号民事判决书); Xinjiang Higher Court (2020) xinminzao 40 (新疆维吾尔自治区高级人民法院 (2020)新民再40号民事判决书).

219 Stoffels, Rn. 264.

220 BGH NJW 1989, 222 (223); Stoffels, Rn. 264; Krause in: Clemenz/Kreft/Krause, Einführung, Rn. 127.

221 Stoll, in: FS Beitzke 1979，759（764 f.).

6.1.2 *The Scope of Incorporation Control: A Broad Meaning*

Incorporation control understood with a narrow meaning is only § 305 II BGB,[222] but incorporation control understood with a broad meaning includes some other regulations of § 305 ff. BGB. For example, the priority of the individually negotiated agreement prescribed by § 305b BGB is also part of incorporation control because this regulation replaces standard business terms with private intent, which is similar § 305 II BGB in terms of legal consequences.[223] As far as the legal consequence of § 305b BGB is concerned, it is not different from the legal implications of content control (§§ 307 ff. BGB).

There is an opinion that the regulation of surprising terms (§ 305c I BGB) is part of incorporation control because of the legal consequence.[224] A different opinion is that a term can be surprising only if it has been effectively incorporated into the contract.[225] In other words, § 305c I BGB is not the same as the other parts of incorporation control. The courts are allowed not to answer the difficult question of whether a standard business term is incorporated effectively (§ 305 II BGB) if the term is surprising.[226]

It is also extremely difficult to distinguish between surprising standard business terms and unreasonable standard business terms (§ 307 BGB).[227] In early German case law the courts declared a "surprising" clause always with consideration of its content.[228] Unreasonable, disadvantageous standard business terms are regularly considered to be surprising.[229] It rarely occurs that a customer is "surprised" by a contractual term, the content of which fully complies with the requirements of §§ 307 ff. BGB.

§ 305c BGB shows the vague boundary between incorporation control and content control even in German law when incorporation control is understood as having a broad meaning.

---

222 Cf. MüKoBGB/Basedow BGB § 305c Rn. 4.
223 Cf. Krause in: Clemenz/Kreft/Krause, Einführung, Rn. 126.
224 Palandt/Heinrichs BGB § 305c Rn. 1, 2.
225 Erman/Roloff/Looschelders BGB § 305c Rn. 6.
226 Cf. MüKoBGB/Basedow BGB § 305c Rn. 1.
227 MüKoBGB/Basedow BGB § 305c Rn. 4.
228 BGHZ 60, 243 (245) = NJW 1973, 990; BGH DB 1975, 2366 (2368); 1976, 1616 f.; cf. BGH NJW 1965, 246; 1969, 230; BGHZ 54, 106 (109) = NJW 1970, 1596; BGH NJW 1978, 945 (947); BB 1983, 1880; OLG Karlsruhe VersR 1971, 158 (160); OLG Hamm BB 1983, 1304 (1307); LG Bielefeld NJW 1973, 1797; MüKoBGB/Basedow BGB § 305c Rn. 4.
229 MüKoBGB/Basedow BGB § 305c Rn. 4.

6.2 The Chinese Law

Although the Chinese Civil Code separates incorporation control and content control, they are still inextricably linked. This link is first shown in the Second Interpretation of the Chinese Contract Law of China's Supreme Court.

6.2.1 The Origin of the Link Between Incorporation Control and Content Control

In Chinese Contract Law, the obligation to provide a reminder and explanation of Art. 39 CCL creates high requirements for the user in theory, but the legal consequences of non-fulfillment of these requirements are not stipulated in Art. 39 CCL. Art. 39 CCL is an incomplete regulation lacking legal consequences. As to how to solve this problem, there is an academic opinion stating that the standard business term should not be subject to content control where the user has fulfilled the obligation of reminder and explanation. The other academic opinion regards the obligation of reminder and explanation as incorporation control, and thus Art. 40 CCL is applicable even after their fulfillment.

The Second Interpretation of the Application of the Chinese Contract Law by the Supreme Court also tried to solve this problem. In this interpretation, Art. 10 states that a standard business term should be declared invalid if the user has reminded the contractual partner that this standard business term exempts or alleviates their liability and the content of this standard business term violates Art. 40 CCL.

Unfortunately, the Chinese Supreme Court does not mention in Art. 10 of this interpretation whether the application of Art. 40 CCL must be premised on the absence of the reminder or an explanation in Art. 39 CCL. However, the courts often misread that Art. 10 of this interpretation creates an additional premise to the application of Art. 40 CCL. This additional premise is the non-fulfillment of the obligation of reminder and explanation in Art. 39 CCL. The practical result of this misreading is that the Chinese courts often make efforts to demonstrate that the user had not reminded the contractual partner of a standard business term or had not explained it to the contractual partner before the contractual conclusion if the Chinese courts want to invalidate the standard business term. In a word, the misreading of the interpretation leads to the unnecessary combination between incorporation control and content control.

6.2.2 *The Continuous Link Between Incorporation Control and Content Control*

Although the Chinese Civil Code replaced Chinese Contract Law making the interpretation of the Supreme Court of China no longer directly applicable, the influence of the above judicial practice continues. For example, where the content of standard business terms is unacceptable, Chinese courts often declare that the user had not drawn the attention of the contractual partner to these standard business terms or had not explained these standard business terms to the contractual partner before the contractual conclusion. Chinese courts often do not check the material content of these standard business terms.[230]

Usually, Chinese judicial rulings discuss the incorporation control and the content control requirements separately. However, it often happens that the obligation of reminder and explanation is not thought to have been fulfilled by the user, according to the rulings, when the content of the clause should be void because its content is unacceptable.[231] Of course, there are also a few judicial cases in which the user has been deemed to have fulfilled the obligation of reminder and explanation, and the court still invalidates the term because of its content.[232] The probability of the occurrence of the former case is far higher than that of the latter case.

The reason for this practice of the Chinese courts may be that it is difficult to extract the applicable criteria for content control from abstract content of Art. 497 CCC (formerly Art. 40 CCL). There is also a consensus surrounding Art. 496 CCC (formerly Art. 39 CCL) that the reminder requirement means marking the terms with special symbols. The Chinese courts are also able to decide, with the help of the burden of proof, the obligation of explanation. Thus, the application of Art. 496 CCC is far more maneuverable than that of Art. 497 CCC.

---

230 See Shanghai First Intermediate Court (2020) hu 01 minzhong 10251 (上海市第一中级人民法院(2020)沪01民终10251号民事判决书); Xinjiang Higher Court (2020) xinminzai 40 (新疆维吾尔自治区高级人民法院 (2020)新民再40号民事判决书).

231 Chongqing First Intermediate Court (2016) yu 01minzhong 7409 (重庆市第一中级人民法院民事判决书(2016)渝01民终7409号); Hebei Yichang Intermediate Court (2016) e 05 minzhong 1572 (湖北省宜昌市中级人民法院民事判决书(2016)鄂05民终1572号).

232 Shanghai First Intermediate Court (2016) hu 01 minzhong 6725 (上海市第一中级人民法院 民事判决书 (2016)沪01民终6725号).

6.3 Summary

There are connections between the incorporation control and the content control rules in both German law and Chinese law. The connection in German law results firstly from procedural economic reasons in the judicial rulings and secondly from § 305b BGB. The connection in Chinese law is based on the interpretation of Art. 39 and 40 CCL of the Supreme Court. This connection continues to exist in Chinese judicial practice because of the lack of clear criteria for content control under Art. 497 CCC.

Chapter 2: The Problem Shared by Germany and China: Differentiating Between B2C Contracts and B2B Contracts

Based on the discussion in Chapter 1, we can see that the differentiating between B2C and B2C standard business terms is a problem shared by Germany and China. In German law, the legislation is differentiated insufficiently, and the case law blurs the boundary between B2B and B2C transactions. In Chinese law, there is no legislative differentiation, but Chinese courts often treat B2B and B2C standard business terms differently. Yet the Chinese judicial differentiation lacks legal certainty. Therefore, a further discussion on how to achieve a proper differentiation between B2C and B2B standard business terms is needed.

1 The Materials for the Analysis of this Problem

The discussions over the differentiation between B2C and B2B contracts in the control of standard business terms are very distinct between Germany and China. The Chinese judicial practice's approaches to differentiation do not seem to be paid enough attention by Chinese academic studies. On the contrary, there are already a number of German academic studies on this problem.

The differentiation between B2C and B2B standard business terms is more complicated in Germany as the German Civil Code has gray lists and blacklists of void standard business terms (§ 308, 309 BGB) and a requirement to consider commercial customs (§ 310 I BGB), both of which do not exist in the Chinese Civil Code. § 308 BGB contains prohibited standard business terms with the possibility of judicial evaluation. § 309 BGB contains prohibited business terms without the possibility of judicial evaluation. According to § 310 I BGB, §§ 308, 309 BGB are not directly applicable to B2C transactions and § 307 BGB theoretically is the only legal basis for content control of B2B standard business terms. Also, according to § 310 I BGB, the courts should consider commercial customs where they apply § 307 BGB to B2B standard business terms.

These differences in academic studies and the legislation suggest that it would be more comprehensive to analyze this problem mainly based on the German literature, and most of the analysis can be applied to the problem in the Chinese Civil Code, except for §§ 308, 309 BGB. The analysis will also refer to §§ 308, 309 BGB where necessary although a full coverage of the prohibitions is unrealistic because of the length, theme and scope of this dissertation.

2 The Reason for the Differentiation Between B2B and B2C Standard Business Terms

The original intention of the unified control of B2C and B2B standard business terms was to prevent the users of standard business terms from unilaterally abusing the freedom of contract.[233] However, with the deeper understanding of the control of standard business terms, economic power inequality,[234] information asymmetry[235] and market failure[236] are also discussed as the purposes of the control of standard business terms. Because B2C transactions are both in line with unilaterally abusing the freedom of contract and the other aforementioned purposes, B2C standard business terms are the undisputed object of judicial control. On the contrary, there are political disputes about whether and how to control B2B standard business terms.[237] In order to figure out an appropriate approach to control B2B standard business terms, we have to observe justifications of the differentiation between B2B and B2C transactions from two perspectives: the need to protect contractual partners facing standard business terms and the special needs of transactions.[238]

2.1 Protection Needs

Because of their inferior position, consumers face considerable risks to their interests compared with other contractual partners facing standard business terms. The law cannot expect consumers to overcome these risks by themselves. Therefore, consumers need special legal protections.[239] The perspective of this protection is based on the legal assumption of average consumers. That means the inferiority of average consumers in terms of intellectual disadvantage[240] and economic strength[241] making it difficult for them to examine standard business terms or to introduce negotiations. Even if standard business terms are understandable to consumers, it is still usually unrealistic for them to introduce negotiations. Because B2C transactions are intended to meet personal, household,

233 Cf. BGH NJW 1971, 1034 (1035).
234 Cf. Lindacher, BB 1972, 296 (297).
235 Cf. Hellwege, S. 553.
236 Cf. Schlösser, Jura 2008, 81 (82).
237 See Chapter 2, part 5 of this dissertation.
238 Cf. Wolf/Pfeiffer § 305, Rn. 120.
239 Cf. Kemper, S. 31.
240 Cf. Baudenbacher, ZBJV 123 (1987), 505 (511).
241 Cf. Hillermeier, BB 1976, 725 (727).

and other similar needs, the introduction of negotiations would bring about transaction costs that are too large.

The inferiority of consumers is not in the expectation of the classic civil law. That is why their legal protection is special. The classic civil law was formed under the background of the liberal economy where the contractual freedom is amplified to the extreme[242] and market forces are indulged.[243] The direct realization of substantive contractual justice is not the goal of classic civil law. In its arrangement, classic civil law expects contractual justice to be achieved through contract freedom. That means both rational sides of the contract should shape and conclude a contract by free self-determined decisions.[244] The freedom of contract guarantees the appropriateness of the contract (Richtigkeit). The balance of the contract is not the main concern of classic civil law.[245]

The above-mentioned theory of classic civil law has a presupposition: both sides of the contract are able to safeguard their own interests and make a rational decision.[246] When the presupposition is not satisfied, additional legal rules are needed to guarantee the exercise of the contractual freedom, or to correct the content of the contract breaching the justice of the contract.

The B2C standard business terms do not satisfy the presupposition due to the economic inferiority of consumers. Moreover, when using standard business terms, enterprises have made careful calculations of their risks, and the consumers, as the contractual partner, do not have the same opportunity and ability to make these calculations, which causes information asymmetry.[247] Because the economic inferiority position of consumers and the asymmetry of information are combined, there is a need for special legal protection for consumers facing standard business terms.

Under normal circumstances, a contractual partner facing a B2B standard business term is considered to have a stronger position and more trading experience than a consumer.[248] The B2B contractual partners should be expected to be familiar with the common standard business terms in their core business[249] and to conduct research on their legal effects when necessary.[250] They are usually

242 Cf. Kemper, S. 33.
243 Cf. Reifner/Michael, S. 14.
244 Cf. Zweigert/ Kötz, 1984, S. 8.
245 Cf. Flume, S.7 f.
246 Cf. Schäfer/Ott, S. 499.
247 Cf. Maier-Reimer/Niemeyer, NJW 2015, 1713 (1716); Leuschner, JZ 2010, 875 (879).
248 Cf. Stoffels, Rn. 552.
249 BGH NJW 1985, 738 (738).
250 Huth, S. 44.

expected to be able to understand the economic significance and risks of standard business terms,[251] especially within their core business. And they are also expected to have the ability to avoid the negative effects brought by the standard business terms.[252]

Under the above premises, a B2B contractual partner is expected to have the ability to offset the aforementioned information asymmetry brought by the unilateral drafting of standard business terms.[253] Therefore, the law will usually assume that a B2B contractual partner has the same obligation to introduce negotiations as a B2B user. If a contractual partner in a B2B transaction gives up the opportunity to negotiate the unilaterally drafted contractual terms, based on the principle of self-responsibility (Selbstverantwortung), the contractual partner should also bear the consequences and not be allowed to rely on legal intervention for protection.[254]

However, the aforementioned is only normal of B2B transactions under certain preconditions. The B2B contractual partners possess ability and experience only in fields where they usually do business, in other words, their core business. That means the B2B contractual partners only have the possibility of possessing a comparable experience and ability to those of the users when both are engaged in the same or overlapping fields for their main source of profit. That also means that a B2B contractual partner facing standard business terms outside its core business deserves higher protection than one within its core business. What is more, even if both parties to the contract are mainly engaged in their core business, there may still be market failures in violation of the assumption of classic civil law so that a B2B contractual partner facing standard business terms cannot make independent decisions freely. Therefore, the protection need of the B2B contractual partners also varies. It is without any doubt that consumers facing standard business terms deserve special protection by the law.[255] And this special protection should possibly be extended to some B2B contractual partners under certain circumstances.

251 Hertel, S. 95.
252 Wolf/Pfeiffer § 307, Rn.186 ff.
253 Cf. Kessel/Jüttner, BB 2008, 1350 (1352).
254 Cf. Hellwege, S. 579.
255 Cf. Wolf/Pfeiffer, § 310, Rn. 3.

2.2 Transaction Needs

Regarding B2C transactions, on the one hand, consumers only have equal status with enterprises in theory in the market economy, but in fact, consumers are unable to fully identify and compare the potential risks hidden behind different standard business terms affiliated with products or services in the market. A consumer's attention is usually only focused on the comparison of apparent qualities and prices rather than standard business terms.

Enterprises are always passing on costs and risks to consumers through standard business terms.[256] The unbalance between enterprises and consumers requires further information disclosure and legal corrections through judicial control.[257] A high degree of private autonomy and self-responsibility (Selbstverantwortung) is needed in the B2B field. In fact, B2B transactions can hardly avoid the pre-formulation and reuse of contractual terms. Based on trading experience and legal knowledge, a B2B contractual partner's calculations of costs and benefits behind standard business terms will foresee possible damages and reduce risks.[258]

In the B2B field, the content of the contract is not always based on negotiations either. A simple distinction between B2B and B2C contracts does not conform to the reality of this field. The use of standard business terms in the B2B field is conducive to saving unnecessary costs through standardization and avoiding the losses caused by employees in drafting contracts.[259] However, these needs of B2B transactions do not mean that all B2B contracts should be subject to the same rules of standard business terms. The circumstances of the market also have an impact on transactions and thus influence the legitimacy of risk aversion and cost saving and create the need for differentiated control of different B2B transactions. Therefore, in terms of transaction needs, there should be different treatments within the B2B field although B2B transactions generally require looser regulations than B2C transactions under normal circumstances.

According to the protection needs of the contractual partner and the needs of the transactions, in the control of standard business terms, it is necessary to distinguish B2C standard business terms from B2B standard business terms and to classify B2B transactions into sub-types so as to distinguish regulations within the B2B field.

256 Cf. Hippel, S. 1 f.
257 Cf. Karatzenis, S. 13.
258 Cf. Kessel/Stomps, BB 2009, 2666 (2675).
259 Lischek/Mahnken, ZIP 2007, 158 (159).

3 The Indicative Effects of §§ 308, 309 BGB

The prohibitions in §§ 308, 309 BGB are a summary of the BGH case law before the AGBG was developed for B2B transactions by means of the judicial evaluation of § 242 BGB.[260] However, when the AGBG was drafted, the legislator did not intend these prohibitions for the control of B2B contracts.[261] The scope of application of these prohibitions thus excludes B2B contracts through § 24 AGBG (now § 310 I 1 BGB), but this regulation does not change the fact that the prohibitions in §§ 308, 309 BGB are typical situations of unreasonable disadvantages to contractual partners.[262] The typical situations of unreasonable disadvantages are still different from an indicative effect that leads to the burden of persuasion on the user to defend the reasonableness of standard business terms. According to the wording of § 310 I BGB, the intention of § 310 I 2 BGB is not to set an "indicative effect" of §§ 308, 309 BGB but only to avoid the wrong understanding of § 310 I 1 BGB so that the void standard business terms listed in §§ 308 and 309 BGB are always valid in B2B transactions.[263]

The BGH goes too far on this issue and follows from the prohibitions in §§ 308, 309 BGB an "indicative effect" for B2B standard business terms.[264] As early as 1984, the BGH affirmed for the first time the indicative effect of the prohibitions in the former § 11 AGBG (now § 309 BGB) for unreasonable disadvantages of B2B standard business terms.[265] According to the case law, a B2B standard business term inadmissible under § 309 BGB constitutes an unreasonable disadvantage under § 307 I BGB as long as it is not justified by the needs of B2B transactions.[266] An exception is that an indicative effect of § 309 No. 9a, c BGB is rejected.[267] This similar indicative effect extends to § 308 BGB, but the possibility of valuation in § 308 BGB reduces the function of presumption resulting from this indicative effect.[268] As a result, the indicative effect often makes the

260 Cf. Bastian/Böhm, BB 1974, 110 (110 ff.).
261 Cf. Rabe, NJW 1987, 1978 (1982).
262 Graf v. Westphalen, NJW 2009, 2977 (2978).
263 Cf. BT-Drs. 7/3919, 43 ff.; BT-Drs. 7/5422, 14.
264 Cf. BGH NJW 2016, 2173, Rn. 30; BGHZ 90, 273 (278) = NJW 1984, 1750 (1751).
265 BGHZ 90, 273 (278) = NJW 1984, 1750 (1751).
266 BGH NJW 2007, 3774 (3775); NJW 1988, 1785 (1788); 1984, 1750 (1751).
267 BGH I WM 2019, 271 Rn. 22; BGH NJW-RR 2012, 626 Rn. 13.
268 BeckOGK/Richters/Friesen BGB § 310 Rn. 53.

intensity of content control almost the same between B2B and B2C contracts under German law.[269]

In spite of the indicative effect, the BGH also admits that §§ 308, 309 BGB are not directly applicable in B2B transactions.[270] This opinion is preferable over the direct applications of §§ 308, 309 BGB to B2B standard business terms. This indirect role of those prohibitions in § 308, 309 BGB means that the courts should carry out a parallel judicial evaluation in the B2B field in spite of the reference to §§ 308, 309 BGB in content control. Additionally, the more economically dependent on the user the contractual partner is, the higher the possibility that §§ 308, 309 BGB are applicable to B2B standard business terms.[271] This indirect role also requires the courts to consider certain circles of contractual partners with special needs of protection even in the B2B transactions, for example, small or medium-sized enterprises.[272] For these contractual partners with special needs of protection, the indirect role of the prohibitions is similar to the so-called indicative effect.

Although the indirect role of the prohibitions exists in the above-mentioned situations, a general extension of the indicative effect to all B2B standard business terms like the present BGH practice should be avoided, especially for the exemptions and restrictions of liabilities, to which the BGH often applies the indicative effect.[273]

In the parallel evaluation, the specific practice in the relevant branch must be taken into account by the courts.[274] In the B2B field, there could be new types of transactions that satisfy the special needs of certain branches. These needs should be considered in the process of judicial valuation in the interpretation of § 307 BGB. For example, if a long-term construction contract including amortization and unconditional guarantee of the quality is invalidated by the court under § 307 BGB, the calculation basis for the financing of such projects could be endangered.[275]

In summary, the indicative effect is not suitable for all standard business terms but only for the contractual partners with special needs for protection. In the

---

269 BeckOGK / Richters / Friesen BGB § 310 Rn. 53; Staudinger/Piekenbrock BGB § 310, Rn. 29.

270 BGH NJW 2007, 3774.

271 Cf. MüKoBGB / Basedow BGB § 310 Rn. 11.

272 Cf. BeckOGK / Richters / Friesen, BGB § 310 Rn. 52.

273 BGH NJW 2007, 3774 (3775).

274 BGH NJW-RR 1997, 1253 (1255); BGHZ 103, 316 = WM 1997, 1817.

275 BGH NJW 2013; 856; MüKoBGB / Basedow BGB § 305 Rn. 13.

control of the other standard business terms, the courts shall undertake a parallel judicial evaluation in the B2B field in spite of the reference to §§ 308, 309 BGB.

4 Arguments for the Looser Control of B2B Standard Business Terms

In Germany, scholars and lawyers have a persuasive voice for changing the civil code and case law, and come up with many suggestions for doing so.[276] An important reason for these calls is to enhance the competitiveness of German law by reducing the restrictions on B2B standard business terms.[277] Another unavoidable reason for promoting the reduction of restrictions on the B2B field by the standard business terms may be that large companies try to exclude the restrictions of the standard business terms in their transactions with suppliers, thereby gaining "freedom of business" and realizing their own interests under the circumstances. Therefore, relevant reforms should not fail to pay attention to competition law, so that reforms of standard business terms do not aggravate market monopoly.

A different consideration can therefore be made by identifying the typical interests of the groups involved and concretizing them to control standards in the form of area and group-specific case groups. It should be emphasized that also for the appropriateness test according to § 307 BGB (i.e., the 2nd stage of the test model proposed by us) it is definitely assumed that there is scope for assessment that allows a significantly stronger differentiation, especially according to branch, group and allow typical business needs.[278]

5 Proposals for Legislative Changes in German Literature

There are a lot of proposals for legislative reforms of the control of standard business terms in Germany. These proposals advocate that the legislators should pay more attention to B2B practice and special needs in the B2B field.[279] These

---

276 Cf. Berger/Kleine BB 2007, 2137; Kessel/Jüttner BB 2008, 1350; Lenkaitis/Löwisch ZIP 2009, 441; Kessel/ Stomps BB 2009, 2666; Berger ZIP 2006, 2149; Graf v. Westphalen NJW 2009, 2977; Verhandlungen des 69. Deutschen Juristentages, München 2012, II/1 S. I 90.; Verhandlungen des 71. Deutschen Juristentages, Essen 2016, II/2, S. K 197, Nr. 26.

277 Cf. Berger NJW 2010, 465 (466); Maier-Reimer/Niemeyer NJW 2015, 1713 (1719); Lischek/Mahnken ZIP 2007, 158 (163).

278 Kessel / Stomps, BB 2009, 2666 (2674 f.).

279 Cf. Huth, S. 118.

proposals can give us inspiration as to how to differentiate between B2C standard business terms and B2B standard business terms on the control. Therefore, this dissertation will introduce these proposals and give comments when necessary.

5.1 Frankfurt Initiative

The Frankfurt Initiative advocates that contractual terms or the entire contract based on the overall autonomous business decisions (selbstbestimmte unternehmerische Entscheidung) of both sides in the B2B field should not be regarded as standard business terms, and the pre-formulated contractual terms at this premise do not need to be changed by either of the parties to the contract to be qualified as individually negotiated terms. However, this rule should not apply to the contractual terms where the contractual partner is a micro corporation under § 267a HGB.[280] This adopts an overall approach, in which the contractual partner's autonomous decision is determined from the perspective of all standard business terms involved in a single transaction. The autonomous business decision here can be proven through a series of indicators (Indizien). These indicators include contractual negotiations (Verhandeln) over a longer period of time, the conclusion of the identical contractual terms in the past, the user's acceptance of contractual changes proposed by the contractual partner, understanding or grossly negligent ignorance of the legal and economic significance of the pre-formulated contractual terms, the involvement of legal consultations and the business size of the contractual partner.[281]

The Frankfurt Initiative also advocates for unreasonableness to be determined differently between the B2C and the B2B field, and argues that a standard business term should only be void if it grossly deviates from good business practice in a manner contrary to good faith.[282]

The Frankfurt Initiative's proposal includes the determination of standard business terms and content control. Part of the determination of standard business terms adopts an overall approach. In the author's opinion, this overall approach is suitable for B2B standard business terms as it leaves B2B

280 Gesetzgebungsvorschlag zur Änderung des AGB-Rechts im unternehmerischen Geschäftsverkehr, 2018. S. 6.

281 Gesetzgebungsvorschlag zur Änderung des AGB-Rechts im unternehmerischen Geschäftsverkehr, 2018. S. 6.

282 https://www.zvei.org/fileadmin/user_upload/Themen/Maerkte_Recht/Allgemeine_Geschaeftsbedingungen_im_unternehmerischen_Geschaeftsverkehr/pdf/AGB-Initiative-Positionspapier-Stand-04-2015.pdf.

transactions enough freedom to shape the whole contract. In addition, part of the criteria for content control is not clear enough for B2B standard business terms. The series of indicators contain both vague factors and definite factors. Among them, the most meaningful factor deserving discussion is the business size of the contractual partner, which often connects to the needs for protection of contractual partners.

5.2 Müller

Müller's suggestion is that a B2B contractual term should be deemed negotiated if the contracting parties have negotiated (verhandelt) it individually or in connection with other terms of the same contract in the appropriate manner for the subject matter of the contract and the circumstances of the contract. In addition, there should be no requirement for the user to change the pre-formulated B2B contractual term in order that it is qualified as an individually negotiated term. However, these rules should not apply if a pre-formulated contractual term is used against a micro-enterprise (§ 267a HGB). The contractual partner is not allowed to invoke its status as a micro-enterprise if the user is unable to identify its status when the contract is concluded.[283] Müller also suggests that B2B standard business terms should be only void if they roughly deviate from a good business practice that is contrary to the requirements of good faith.[284]

Part of the definition of standard business terms of Müller's suggestion is quite similar to the Frankfurt Initiative's proposal. Thus, they share similar advantages and disadvantages on the part of the definition. As for the part of content control, Müller's suggestion relies too much on "good business practice" which provides no clear path for judicial practice.

5.3 Berger

Another suggestion, from Berger, about the determination of negotiations, is that a contractual term in a B2B contract should be deemed to have been negotiated if both sides have negotiated (verhandelt) it in an appropriate manner for the subject of the contract and the circumstances of the conclusion of the contract individually or in connection with other terms in the same contract.[285]

283 Müller IWRZ 2018, 153 (160).
284 Müller IWRZ 2018, 153 (160).
285 Berger NJW 2010, 465 (470).

Berger's suggestion also refers to the business customs in § 310 BGB but adds the circumstances of B2B transactions to be considered, and notes that a B2B contractual partner is less vulnerable than a consumer.[286]

Berger's suggestion about the determination of negotiations also adopts an overall approach. What is worth mentioning is his suggestion concerning content control which underlines the difference in the need for protection between B2B and B2C transactions and points out the basis of the differentiation between the control of B2B and B2C standard business terms.

5.4 Müller/Griebeler/Pfeil

There is a suggestion to enumerate a series of circumstances, made by Müller/Griebeler/Pfeil, to set up a rebuttable presumption that a pre-formulated contractual term is already negotiated (ausgehandelt). These circumstances include the negotiation (Verhandlung) of longer than two months between the two sides of a contract, the contractual partner having commented at least once on the contractual draft, the value of the transaction being at least 1 million euros, the contractual partner having been advised by a lawyer when concluding the contract, the contractual partner having implemented at least one amendment to the proposed contractual terms, and the contractual terms essentially conforming with the contract negotiated earlier between the user and the contractual partner.[287]

Müller/Griebeler/Pfeil also suggests replacing the commercial customs in § 310 BGB with the needs of B2B contractual partners for protection.[288]

Like the proposal of the Frankfurt Initiative, the suggestion made by Müller/Griebeler/Pfeil highlights indicators for the definition of standard business terms. One of these indicators is the value limit of 1 million euro, which deserves further discussion.[289]

5.5 Lawyers' Assembly

The 2012 Lawyers' Assembly recommendation was to replace "aushandeln" with "verhandeln" and to consider the contractual terms already negotiated by both sides in a previous contract as no longer qualifying as standard business terms when they are used again in a new contract between the same parties.[290] This

286 Berger NJW 2010, 465 (470).
287 Müller/Griebeler/Pfeil BB 2009, 2658 (2662).
288 Müller/Griebeler/Pfeil BB 2009, 2658.
289 See Chapter 4, part 2.4 of this dissertation.
290 Stellungnahme Nr. 23/2012, Verbesserung der Wettbewerbsfähigkeit deutschen

proposal also requires the contractual partner to proceed with the negotiation actively. Otherwise, the contractual partner is not allowed to invoke § 307 I, II BGB to invalidate the standard business terms.[291]

The Lawyers' Assembly also advocates that there should be no unreasonable disadvantage within the meaning of § 307 I, II if a standard business term does not significantly deviate from reasonable business practice (vernünftige unternehmerische Praxis) taking into account the overall content of the contract and the circumstances accompanying the conclusion of the contract as well as the circumstances of the industry concerned.[292]

The concept "reasonable business practice" in the recommendation of the lawyers' assembly is so unclear as it the other concept "verhaneln" used by this recommendation. It is also too rigid to impose the obligation to proceed with the negotiation actively on all B2B contractual partners without a classification based on their concrete needs for protection.

5.6 Huth

Huth recommends that § 310 BGB should clearly stipulate the need for it to be presumed that standard business terms are unreasonably disadvantageous to the contractual partner when the standard business terms are commonly used in relevant fields of B2B transactions.[293]

Huth's proposal to differentiate between standard business terms and individually negotiated terms is that all contract terms of a B2B contract should be considered as having been negotiated as long as the main obligations of the B2B contract fall within the core business of the contractual partner, if the user has given the contractual partner an opportunity before the contractual conclusion to exert influence over the overall content of the contractual terms, and if the changes of the content required by the contractual partner lead to appropriate amendments to the respective contractual terms.[294]

Rechts durch Änderung des AGB-Rechts für den unternehmerischen Verkehr v. 20.03.2012.

291 Stellungnahme Nr. 23/2012, Verbesserung der Wettbewerbsfähigkeit deutschen Rechts durch Änderung des AGB-Rechts für den unternehmerischen Verkehr v. 20.03.2012.

292 Stellungnahme Nr. 23/2012, Verbesserung der Wettbewerbsfähigkeit deutschen Rechts durch Änderung des AGB-Rechts für den unternehmerischen Verkehr. v. 20.03.2012.

293 Huth S. 348.

294 Huth, S. 347.

In the author's opinion, the commonly used standard business terms and the core business of the contractual partner in Huth's proposal are useful concepts for differentiating between B2B and B2C standard business terms on the control. However, there are still too many restrictions of the definition of individually negotiated terms within the core business of contractual partners.[295] Overall, the differentiation between B2B and B2C standard business terms in Huth's proposal is not comprehensive enough because it is not based on a classification of B2B transactions corresponding to the needs for protection of contractual partners.[296]

5.7 Stomps

On the differentiation between individual terms and standard business terms, Stomps recommends that a B2B contractual term should be considered a standard business term if the self-decision of the contractual partner was significantly impaired when the contract was concluded. This is especially so, if the contractual partner is economically dependent on the user of the clause, or the contractual partner had no reasonable opportunity to understand the effects of the term. And if the contract price exceeds 500,000 euro, it should be assumed that there is no impairment to the self-decision of the contractual partner.[297]

Stomps also made a proposal about content control, suggesting that the unreasonableness of B2B standard business terms could be caused by the imbalance of contractual content in individual cases rather than only from the general perspective. And as far as the B2B standard business terms of liability exemption are concerned, Stomps recommends that the courts should take into account whether: the term is common in B2B transactions or in the specific sector, whether there are available insurance options, and whether the disruption of the balance between the two sides can be compensated by another contractual term in this contractual term.[298]

5.8 Axer

Axer suggests that pre formulated contractual terms should not be considered standard business terms insofar as they are expressions of the self-determined decisions of both sides.[299] If B2B contractual terms are within the core business

295 See Chapter 4, part 3.2.1.1 of this dissertation.
296 See Chapter 4, part 3.1 of this dissertation.
297 Stomps, S. 321.
298 Stomps, S. 321.
299 Axer, S. 277.

of the contractual partner, they should be presumed to be self-decision of both sides even if the contractual partner does not make any suggestions concerning changes of the content on the premise that the user had made these contractual terms available to the contractual partner and had expressed the willingness to accept changes before the contractual conclusion. If the B2B contractual partner suggests changes to the contractual terms, a self-decision is presumed if the parties have negotiated (verhandelt) in an appropriate manner about every individual contractual term or the contract as a whole. There is no need to change the pre-formulated content of the standard business terms by transforming them into individually negotiated terms.[300]

For B2B standard business terms belonging to the core business of the contractual partner, the peculiarities of the type of transactions and the generally lower needs for protection of the contractual partners in the B2B field than that of consumers in the valuation under of § 307 I BGB should always be considered appropriately.[301]

The most valuable part of Axer's suggestion is its introduction of the core business into the balance of protection needs of the contractual partner. As for the determination of negotiations, Axer's core idea is the free self-decision of both sides, an enlightening point.

5.9 Leuschner, Hannemann, Kieninger and Graf von Westphalen

Leuschner proposes that the B2B standard business terms limiting negligent liability should be allowed under a certain value if the user has a sufficient incentive to act carefully despite this limitation, and the user has referred his contractual partner in a suitable manner to this limitation of liability.[302]

Leuschner also proposes a value limitation for invoking an exemption from the control of standard business terms: if the price of the contract is at least 1 million euro, § 305c and §§ 307 f. BGB should not apply unless the contractual partner is dependent on the user due to the relatively stronger market power of the user.[303]

Another proposal, made by Hannemann, recommends making it clear that entrepreneurs need less protection than consumers, and a breach of the §§ 308,

---

300 Axer, S. 277.
301 Axer, S. 281.
302 Cf. Leuschner, ZIP 2015, 1045.
303 Cf. Leuschner, ZIP 2015, 1045.

309 BGB can only lead to the invalidity of B2B standard business terms in exceptional cases.[304]

Kieninger's proposal concerns indicators for the determination of individually negotiated terms. These indicators include: that the transaction is a cross-border transaction, that the contractual price is higher than a certain sum, and that the scale of the contractual partner is so large that there is no need for the control of standard business terms.[305] With one of the above indicators, the contract should be excluded from the control of standard business terms.

Graf von Westphalen suggests that it is not necessary for the determination of negotiations in B2B transactions based on the criterion that the user places the entire non-statutory core content of the contractual terms at the disposal of his contractual partner. The user should be allowed to prove the existence of a negotiation sufficiently, with the fact that they have changed a pre-formulated term significantly at the request of the contractual partner.[306]

Leuschner's proposal to set a contractual value exemption from the control, is widely discussed and will be analyzed further in this dissertation. Hannemann's proposal to refer to different needs for protection between B2C and B2B transactions is similar to Berger's proposal. The method adopted by Kieninger's proposal for the determination of the individually negotiated terms is similar to Müller/Griebeler/Pfeil's proposal, both of which have introduced indicators despite their indicators not being the same.

6 Summary and Evaluation

These proposals can be classified into three categories: indicators, criteria, and the exclusion of specific kinds of transactions. The indicators are circumstances to prove the existence of the negotiation. An example for the exclusion of specific kinds of transactions is Leuschner's proposal concerning whether contractual terms are subject to the control of standard business terms by setting a contractual value limit for the exemption from the control.

The setting of criteria means using the business practice in the B2B field to judge the reasonableness of standard business terms and thereby reduce the level of control over standard business terms. For example, Huth uses common standard business terms in the sector as the criterion for judging reasonableness. The exclusion of special kinds of transactions means excluding some transactions

304 Hannemann AnwBl 2012, 314 (317).
305 Kieninger AnwBl 2012, 301 (304).
306 Graf von Westphalen, ZIP 2015, 1316 (1326).

from the scope of control based on the status of the contractual partner or on other factors of the transaction. For example, the Frankfurt Initiative excludes the transactions, the contractual partners of which are micro-enterprises. And Huth excludes those transactions with contract partners outside of the core business.

In fact, the exclusion of special contractual partners or transactions, or further, the classification of contractual partners or transactions targeted by the control of standard business terms, should be the first step in building differentiated paths for the control of standard business terms in the B2B field. Within the B2B field, different contract partners have different protection needs due to specific circumstances such as transaction background. Different protection needs mean that, without the differentiation between B2B transactions, the indicators or criteria cannot meet the protection needs of contractual partners. Different protection needs are the prerequisites for setting indicators or criteria appropriately.

The setting of specific indicators and criteria is largely a matter of law and policy. In academic discussions, it is difficult to achieve a perfect academic answer because the pursuit of less interference in the B2B field, comprehensive protection for contract partners, and certainty of the rules are difficult to balance. Therefore, this dissertation does not intend to make a new proposal but focuses on the classification of transactions and respective control intensity.

These proposals include three essential points: (a) the demarcation between standard business terms (subject to control) and individually negotiated agreements (not subject to control); (b) making the standard business terms control dependent on the value of the transaction and, (c) a more flexible criterion for judicial control under § 307 BGB is discussed, in which judicial control could be adapted to the needs for protection in transactions.[307]

The German proposals have similarities and differences if we compare them with the relevant Chinese practice over the control of B2B contracts. A similarity is that Chinese courts also have a tendency to deny identifying a contractual term as a standard business term with no concrete explanation.[308] Chinese judicial practice usually lacks indicators for differentiating between standard business terms and individually negotiated terms in the B2B field. An exception

307 MüKoBGB/Basedow BGB § 310 Rn. 24 ff.

308 The Supreme Court of China, (2018) zuigaofamminxiazhong 355 (最高人民法院民事裁定书(2018)最高法民辖终355号); The Supreme Court of China, (2015) zuigaofamminerzhong 381 (最高人民法院民事裁定书(2015)民二终字第381号).

is that a few Chinese courts are trying to set up indicators although they are not commonly accepted judicial opinions in the majority of Chinese courts.[309]

At the level of content control, the too-wide scope of Chinese incorporation control has replaced content control of B2B standard business terms to a large degree.[310] Content control of B2B standard business terms is thus not often enforced. At the same time, Chinese courts also minimize the intensity of incorporation control of B2B standard business terms by concentrating on the special marks of standard business terms with a major interest of the contractual partner.[311] There is still no systematic discussion on the role of the value of the transaction or on more flexible criteria for content control of B2B standard business terms.

309 See Jiangsu Higher Court, (2016) suminshen 612 (江苏省高级人民法院民事裁定书(2016)苏民申 612 号).

310 See Shanghai First Intermediate Court, (2020) hu 01 minzhong 10251 (上海市第一中级人民法院(2020)沪 01 民终 10251 号民事判决书); Xinjiang Higher Court, (2020) xinminzai 40 (新疆维吾尔自治区高级人民法院 (2020)新民再 40 号民事判决书).

311 See Chapter 1, part 3.2.2 of this dissertation.

Chapter 3: The Unique Problem of the Chinese Civil Code and Its German Solution: The Typical Criteria of Content Control

Compared with the German Civil Code, the control of standard business terms in the Chinese Civil Code faces a special problem: the lack of criteria for content control, which is already shown in Chapter 1 of this dissertation.[312] The analysis of the German regulations concerning content control in Chapter 1 of this dissertation also provides the promise of being able to use the German legal experience to solve this problem. To achieve this aim, a further discussion of this problem will take place in this chapter.

1 The Function and Positioning of Art. 497 CCC in Comparison With §§ 307 ff. BGB

1.1 A Comparison Between Art. 497 CCC and §§ 307 ff. BGB

When discussing the positioning and function of Art. 497 CCC, Chinese scholars often compare it with §§ 307 ff. BGB.

Opinions in earlier studies believed that Art. 40 CCL (the predecessor of Art. 497 CCC) was similar to § 309 BGB as both of them contain a list of prohibited standard business terms.[313] Art. 497 CCC limits its own scope of application, only prohibiting unreasonable standard business terms when making revisions of Art. 40 CCL. When drawing a comparison between them, it is not difficult to see that Art. 40 CCL or Art. 497 CCC are in fact not as concrete as § 309 or § 308 BGB. Therefore, the analogy between Art. 40 CCL or Art. 497 and § 309 or § 308 BGB is not suitable.

Another opinion in a later Chinese academic study over Art. 497 CCC is that Art. 497 CCC is similar to § 307 I BGB and that the circumstances for invalidity enumerated in Art. 497 CCC should be collectively considered as unreasonable disadvantages to the contractual partner.[314] According to this opinion, the concrete circumstances for invalidity enumerated by Art. 497 CCC are not important. Chinese courts only have to determine whether a certain standard business

312 See Chapter 1, part 4.2 of this dissertation.

313 SU Haopeng, p. 266

314 See Chapter 5, Part 1 of this dissertation.

term constitutes an unreasonable disadvantage to the contractual partner and do not need to consider which circumstance for invalidity is applicable in a concrete case.

In the author's opinion, the viewpoints mentioned above have not given sufficient consideration to the concrete content of Art. 497 CCC or the development from Art. 40 CCL to Art. 497 CCC. Each circumstance enumerated in Art. 497 CCC has a wider scope of application, more abstract content, and more spaces for judicial evaluation than those of each prohibition in § 308 or 309 BGB.

The history of Art. 497 CCC shows that this provision was legislated on the basis of amendments to Art. 40 CCL. Compared with Art. 40 CCL, the number of circumstances increases, and these circumstances are divided and put into two different sub-items under Art. 40 CCL. Art. 497 No. 2 CCC also requires that the reasonableness of standard business terms is checked, which also makes the circumstances for invalidity different from Art. 40 CCL. That additionally shows that the Chinese legislator believes that there should be differences between the applications of Art. 497 No. 2 and of No. 3 CCC since Art. 497 No. 3 CCC does not mention checking the reasonability of standard business terms.

As for the comparison between § 307 I BGB and Art. 497 CCC, the author does not recognize their similarity. The main content of § 307 I BGB is good faith and unreasonable disadvantages, both of which are the concepts related to uncertainty. The circumstances for invalidity within Art. 497 CCC are much more concrete than in § 307 I BGB. Therefore, Art. 497 CCC is hardly similar to § 307 I BGB. If we look for a regulation in §§ 307 ff. BGB that has a similar positioning and function to Art. 497 CCC, the only possible option is § 307 II BGB.

1.2 The Comparison Between Art. 497 CCC and § 307 II BGB

Art. 497 No. 2, 3 CCC and § 307 II BGB are similar in their degree of concretization and their relation to the general legal principle (fairness or good faith). They are both initial concretizations of the general legal principle.[315] The similarity means that the Chinese interpretation of Art. 497 No. 2, 3 CCC can borrow from the German experience under § 307 II BGB.

The differences between Art. 497 No. 2, 3 CCC and § 307 II BGB should not be ignored either. In the Chinese Civil Code, the general legal principle governing the control of standard business terms is fairness rather than good faith (Art. 496 CCC).[316] However, it is not meaningful to differentiate between fairness

315 See Chapter 1, part 4.2.2 of this dissertation.
316 See HUANG Wei, p. 956.

and good faith. Only the legislator can decide which of them should be imposed on the control of standard business terms.

Another difference between them is that § 307 II BGB provides clearer criteria to apply to the standard business terms in questions. More specifically, § 307 II BGB introduces default rules and the purpose of the contract into the content control process by means of legal interpretation, but Art. 497 CCC does not specify what criteria the courts should apply in practice.

The third difference is that the importance of Art. 497 CCC is distinct from that of § 307 II BGB. This difference is connected to the direction of its interpretation and thus receives a more detailed analysis in the following section.

1.2.1 The Similarity and Connection Between Art. 497 CCC and § 307 II BGB

Art. 497 CCC and § 307 II BGB should both provide legal criteria for content control as they are both initial concretizations of the general legal principle.[317] The concretization in § 307 II BGB is apparently more successful than that in Art. 497 CCC. The deviation from default rules and the jeopardization of the purpose of the contract under § 307 II BGB help German courts to find applicable rules or develop new rules for content control.[318] Chinese courts also need this experience of § 307 II BGB in the application of Art. 497 CCC because the circumstances for the invalidity of standard business terms need further clarification. Courts also need further instructions in order to find applicable legal rules or to be able to develop new rules for content control. In Art. 497 CCC, the core concept of all the circumstances for invalidity of standard business terms is the "liability" or "main right." In order to find out what the "liability" and the "main right" are, respectively, it is crucial to make the criteria clear for content control. The default rules and the purpose of the contract may provide help in determining what the "liability" and the "main right" in Art. 497 CCC are because the default rules and the purpose of the contract are possible sources of the "liability" and the "main right."[319]

317 See Chapter 1, part 4.2.2 of this dissertation.
318 See Chapter 1, part 4.1.2 and 4.1.3 of this dissertation.
319 See Chapter 5, part 3 of this dissertation.

1.2.2 *The Difference and Connection Between Art. 497 CCC and § 307 II BGB*

The roles of default rules and the purpose of contract could be more important for content control in the Chinese Civil Code than in the German Civil Code because of a third difference. The third difference is that Art. 497 CCC is the only legal basis for content control in the Chinese Civil Code while § 307 II BGB plays only a supporting role among the regulations found in §§ 307 ff. BGB. In the German Civil Code, the prohibitions of standard business terms are concretely listed in §§ 308, 309 BGB. § 307 BGB plays only a supporting role and thus is the last in the sequence of application.[320] That is why the German Civil Code is quite rich in content control tools, whereas there is no legal regulation similar to § 307 I BGB in the Chinese Civil Code. There is no blacklist or gray list similar to §§ 308, 309 BGB either. That means Art. 497 CCC is much more important for content control in Chinese law than § 307 I or II BGB in German law. Thus, the introduction of criteria into the content control rules based on Art. 497 CCC is a vital mission of the legal interpretation, in the process of which § 307 II BGB can provide guidance.

1.2.3 *The Differentiation Between Deviations from Default Rules and Jeopardizing the Purpose of Contract*

From a practical angle, default rules and the purpose of the contract under § 307 II Nr. 1 and Nr. 2 BGB are the tools to analyze the reasonableness of standard business terms. They are used to compare the content of a concrete standard business term with existing legal rules, or a rule developed by the courts.[321]

The functions of deviations from default rules and of jeopardizing the purpose of the contract are distinct.[322] Deviations from default rules are a criterion for content control where there is an applicable legislative default rule or an applicable default rule in case law. On the contrary, the jeopardizing of the purpose of a contract plays a role for the courts to develop rules where there are no such rules in the legislation or the case law.[323]

However, there is literature believing that § 307 II Nr. 1 and Nr. 2 BGB can overlap each other in terms of their scopes of applications.[324] It is inherently

320 Cf. Erman/Roloff/Looschelders Vorbemerkung vor § 307 BGB, Rn. 1.
321 See Chapter 1, part 4.1.3.1 of this dissertation.
322 Soergel/Stein § 9 AGBG Rn 41; Hoyningen-Huene, Rn. 281.
323 See Chapter 1, part 4.1.3.1 of this dissertation.
324 See Chapter 1, part 4.1.3.1 of this dissertation.

possible to find overlaps between deviations from default rules and jeopardizing the purpose of the contract when we only focus on the illustrations of the two concepts of default rules and the purpose of the contract. This is because a deviation from a default rule that contains a fair distribution of rights and obligations, possibly also jeopardizes the purpose of contract, especially when the deviation is serious. Also, a contractual term that jeopardizes the purpose of the contract could at the same time, can also deviate from a default rule.

This sequence of applications guarantees the legal certainty. It should also reflect in the differentiation of application between § 307 II Nr. 1 and Nr. 2 BGB. § 307 II Nr. 1 BGB should have the applicable priority over Nr. 2 in order to make sure the courts are not allowed to make use of the large scope of judicial evaluation under Nr. 2 when there is already a relevant default rule to apply. This applicable sequence will avert Nr. 1 and Nr. 2 from overlapping with each other. This is the same as what the pure illustrations of the concepts of default rules and the purpose of contract would lead to.[325] This sequence of applications guarantees the legal certainty. It should also reflect in the differentiation of application between § 307 II Nr. 1 and Nr. 2 BGB. § 307 II Nr. 1 BGB should have the applicable priority over Nr. 2 in order to make sure the courts are not allowed to make use of the large scope of judicial evaluation under Nr. 2 when there is already a relevant default rule to apply. This applicable sequence will avert Nr. 1 and Nr. 2 from overlapping with each other. This is the same as what the pure illustrations of the concepts of default rules and the purpose of contract would lead to.

The above differentiation between deviations from default rules and jeopardizing the purpose of contract is not only meaningful to the application of § 307 II BGB but also makes the two criteria more practical so that the interpretation of Art. 497 CCC may borrow from the experience of the German courts. This is because content control under Art. 497 CCC also has a strong need for criteria for content control and legal certainty.

2 An Analysis of Art. 497 CCC

2.1 Textual Deficits

The legislative model adopted by Art. 497 CCC that is based on the "liability" and "main right" does not directly provide clear criteria for the judicial content control of standard business terms.[326]

325 See Chapter 1, part 4.1.3.1 of this dissertation.
326 See MA Ning, ZWFX 2015 no. 5, p. 1250.

Art. 497 CCC is very vague in its expressions. Standard business terms often fall within its scope of application because it is not unusual that a standard business term has an effect of excluding or limiting the contractual partner's right or liability. But it is impossible for Chinese courts to declare every standard business term with this effect void. Chinese courts urgently need criteria to judge the reasonableness of standard business terms. Here, the aforementioned default rules and the purpose of contract can provide help. Therefore, it is not surprising that some Chinese literature is also making efforts to introduce default rules and the purpose of contract into content control in Chinese law although these efforts are still not connected to the interpretation of Art. 497 CCC.[327]

2.2 Problems in Practice

There have been a large number of judicial cases concerning content control of standard business terms in Chinese judicial practice (before and after the Chinese Civil Code came into force).[328]

In most of these cases[329], Chinese courts avoid comparing the legislative circumstances for invalidity in Art. 497 CCC with the concrete content of standard business terms in question to find out whether the standard business terms conform to one of the circumstances of invalidity. The real impact of Art. 497 CCC in these judicial cases is only that declaration that the courts are authorized by the legislation to invalidate standard business terms.[330] As for what the real meaning of the circumstances for invalidity in Art. 497 CCC is, Chinese courts do not give any explanations.

The reason why Chinese courts often avert from the direct application of the legislative circumstances is that the scope of Art. 497 CCC (or Art. 40 CCL) is so wide that almost all disputed standard business terms have the chance to be

327 For example see GAO Shengping, HNSD 2005, no. 3, p. 75; QI Chunyi, ZWFX 2013, no. 3, p. 653.

328 More than 80,000 judicial decisions can be found on the Chinalawinfo: http:en.pku law.cn.

329 For example, Jiangsu Court 2018, No. 6 p. 23–26 (参见朱柏舟诉诺菲尔健身公司服务合同纠纷案，《江苏省高级人民法院公报》2018 年第 6 辑总第 60 辑，第 23–26 页).

330 See Beijing Third Intermediate Court (2020) jing 03 minzhong 14658 (北京市第三中级人民法院(2020)京 03 民终 14658 号民事判决书)；Hunan Zhuzhou Intermediate Court (2020), xiang 02 minzhong 2135 (湖南省株洲市中级人民法院 (2020)湘 02 民终 2135 号民事判决书)。.

invalidated based on one of the circumstances in Art. 497 CCC.[331] The broad meanings of these circumstances for invalidity in Art. 497 CCC make it difficult for Chinese courts to find any clear criteria to apply concerning content control. In fact, Chinese courts usually only use Art. 497 CCC to declare their judicial power for content control. Chinese courts will not be able to judge the validity of a standard business term based on any of the circumstances for invalidity in Art. 497 CCC if the legal interpretation is not able to introduce real criteria for the content control process. This lack of criteria also makes judicial rulings on the issue of content control unpredictable and leads to legal uncertainty.[332]

3 Summary

Content control in the German Civil Code is the most important reference for Chinese legal studies on this issue. The German Civil Code has a complete system of rules in §§ 307 ff. BGB while the Chinese Civil Code has only Art. 497 CCC as the legal basis for content control. Art. 497 CCC has a similar function to that of § 307 II BGB which contains two sets of criteria for content control: the deviation from default rules and the jeopardizing of the purpose of the contract. Compared with § 307 II BGB, the wording of Art. 497 CCC is too vague to provide criteria for content control, and this leads to problems of legal uncertainty in Chinese legal practice. An analysis of this problem suggests that the introduction of criteria in § 307 II BGB could be a possible solution.

331 See LIANG Huixing, 2014, p. 112.

332 For the same standard business terms, there are often opposite judicial decisions, for example, Shandong Higher Court 2014 luminti 313 (山东省高级人民法院民事判决书(2014)鲁民提字第313号) and Shandong Higher Court 2015 luminti 96 (山东省高级人民法院民事判决书(2015)鲁民提字第96号).

Chapter 4: A Frame for the Differentiation Between the Control of B2C and B2B Standard Business Terms

In order to solve the problem analyzed by chapter 2 of this dissertation, how to differentiate between the control of B2C and of B2B standard business terms, a frame for differentiating between the control of B2C and of B2B standard business terms will be discussed in this chapter. This frame is comprised of general ideas for the direction of legal interpretation of the relevant regulations and also possibly for legislative changes in the future. The core of this frame seeks to classify B2B transactions into different groups based on some factors to be considered that influence the contractual partner's ability to make decisions independently (self-determined decisions) over the conclusion of a contract comprising of or containing standard business terms.

1 Economic and Political Considerations

Differentiating between the control of B2C and B2B standard business terms is unavoidably an economic and political issue. Behind the assumption of the inferior position of contractual partners facing standard business terms is the protection of their economic and political concerns. This protection of contractual partners re-balances market positions and economic strength. The justification of this protection from control of standard business terms needs to be demonstrated economically or politically for every individual contractual partner. This protection from control of standard business terms is already widely accepted for B2C transactions as consumer protection. The picture of B2B transactions is totally different. The above demonstration should be made for every B2B transaction to justify the control of standard business terms. In order to simplify this demonstration, the control of B2B standard business terms requires a classification of transactions to differentiate B2B standard business from with distinct needs of protection.

As an economic and political question, how to differentiate between the control of B2C and B2B standard business terms and how to differentiate the control within B2B standard business terms does not have an absolutely correct answer. This is especially true considering the different economic systems and political ideas that exist between countries. Therefore, as a comparative legal study, this dissertation is not committed to finding a solely correct answer or even a concrete legislative proposal. This dissertation is dedicated to building a framework for analysis for the differentiating between the control of B2C and B2B standard business terms. The basic method of this framework is to classify B2B transactions into those requiring enhanced control and those not requiring enhanced control and compare them with B2C transactions respectively.

2 Factors to Be Considered for the Differentiation of Different Types of B2B Transactions

Most of the factors in this part have been more or less referred to in the literature, but a comprehensive, deep, and systematic frame is still in need. The justifications for the inclusion of the factors into this frame are equally as important as how to determine whether the factors exist. A free decision to conclude a contract by the contractual partner requires no protection of law.

2.1 Core Business

Consumers generally need a higher level of protection than B2B contractual partners.[333] Compared with consumers, B2B contractual partners' abilities to eliminate the negative effects of standard business terms are not the same. Their familiarity with standard business terms is one of the aspects affecting their abilities to eliminate these negative effects. This ability contributes to the free decision to conclude a contract.

The familiarity with standard business terms only applies to business fields that the B2B contractual partners frequently engage in and not those that they rarely take part in.[334] The fields where B2B contractual partners frequently engage are their core business fields. Within their core business, B2B contractual partners often face the same or similar terms and thus have enough relevant trading experience. Within their core business, B2B contractual partners also have an incentive to look into the standard business terms to decide whether to accept them since the core business is the main source of their business earnings. The costs to check the standard business terms and for the introduction of negotiations are, therefore, usually proportional to their earnings from their core business. The saving of such costs is not justified as it would make contractual partners who do not check B2B standard business terms win price advantages in the competition against those contractual partners who will check B2B standard

333 See Chapter 2, part 2.1 of this dissertation.
334 Cf. Uusitalo, S. 164.

business terms in future transactions with end consumers. In B2B transactions, the aforementioned experience, ability, and incentive of the contractual partners can offset the information advantage of the users obtained through their unilateral drafting of standard business terms.[335]

On the contrary, when the contractual partner is outside its core business, the aforementioned experience, ability, and incentive are not comparable to those of the user in its own core business field. That makes the contractual partner weaker in the transaction and thus has the need for protection. This type of transaction between the user in its core business and the contractual partner outside its core business is therefore similar to a B2C transaction. An example is the renting of offices.[336] Therefore, when both parties to the B2B standard business terms are in their core business field, we can call this type of contract a "normal B2B contract." And where only the contractual partner is acting in their core business, the contract can be called a "B2C-like contract." That is because the drafting of standard business terms provides an opportunity for the user to achieve their interests, which cannot be balanced by the experience, ability, or incentive of the contractual partner. This relationship between the user and the contractual partner is like that between the user and the consumer in a B2C transaction.

For B2C-like contracts, a regulatory approach similar to that of B2B contracts should be applied. As a prerequisite, the courts should first judge whether the contract in question is a B2C-like contract. The emphasis here is usually to check whether this contract belongs to part of the contractual partner's core business. Determining whether the B2B contract in question is part of the core business of the contractual partner, should consider whether the transaction is necessary for the business purpose, the frequency of this kind of transaction, and the proportion of this kind of transaction to the contractual partner's earnings.[337] An important indication to attribute a B2B contract to the core business is that the main performance obligation of the contract belongs to part of the business registration.[338] If the contractual partner is an unregistered freelancer, the core business includes all relevant transactions without the purpose of consumption. The determination in concrete cases can also consider the obligations described in offers or advertisements. If a B2B contract involves multiple fields, the judgment should be based on the focus of the contract.[339]

335 Cf. Axer, S. 136.
336 Cf. BGH NJW 2005, 2006.
337 Huth, S. 324.
338 Huth, S. 324.
339 Cf. Huth, S. 324.

Even if a B2B contractual partner concludes a contract as part of its core business, it does not mean that it is able to conclude this contract freely. Other factors such as transaction costs and market position will determine whether the contractual partner is free to accept, change or deny standard business terms. Whether a B2B contractual partner has the ability to freely make a contractual conclusion still depends on the consideration of other transaction-related factors.

2.2 Small and Medium-Sized Enterprises

There are many advocates for stronger the protection of small and medium-sized enterprises in the control of standard business terms.[340] Small and medium-sized enterprises should not receive the same protection as consumers, but they deserve stronger protection than large enterprises.[341] In some German judicial rulings, small and medium-sized enterprises are indeed specially protected. For example, the courts found that the standard business term for additional loan processing fees in contracts with small and medium-sized enterprises should be void because small and medium-sized enterprises are in a comparably inferior position vis-à-vis the banks.[342] This judicial opinion is in line with the academic opinions advocating for the stronger protection of small and medium-sized enterprises taking into account their economic and intellectual inferiority which, in this respect, is to some extent similar to consumers.[343]

The connection between the size of enterprises and transaction costs can also justify the stronger protection of small and medium-sized enterprises. The control of standard business terms has the function of protecting market mechanisms.[344] In the market, the decisive factor that affects the conclusion of the contract is the price and quality of the product or service[345] rather than standard business terms. When the transaction costs to negotiate the terms (reading standard business terms, legal consultations, etc.) are too high[346] and disproportionate to the profits from the transaction, the contractual partners will not even

340 Graf v. Westphalen ZIP 2010, 1110(1115); Schäfer BB 2012, 1231 (1232); Herrmann/Lasch DRiZ 2018, 218 (220).

341 Matthias/Johannes, S. 298.

342 LG Magdeburg, 13.8.15—11 O 1887/14 (689) Rn. 37; LG Neuruppin, 24.9.15—5 O 66/15 Rn. 25–34; LG Düsseldorf, 18.12.2015—10 O 517/14 Rn. 48–49.

343 Cf. Berger, NJW 2010, 465; Müller/Griebeler/Pfeil, BB 2009, 2658.

344 Cf. Bernuth, BB 1999, 1284 (1285).

345 Cf. Palandt/Grüneberg vor § 305, Rn. 6.

346 Cf. Schäfer/Ott, S. 514 f.

read the standard business terms.[347] Due to the disproportion between transaction costs and profits, all market competition between products or services will happen only on their prices and quality rather than on standard business terms. As a consequence, there is usually a market failure in this regard, and the content of standard business terms deteriorates for contractual partners.[348] This deterioration makes the control of standard business terms inevitable even within the core business of the B2B contractual partner.[349]

Transaction costs being too high, alone cannot justify contractual partners being allowed to just ignore standard business terms and make themselves believe there is no unacceptable content in them. If this ignorance is justified and the standard business terms are thus subject to a highly strict level of content control, the high costs saved by the contractual partner will be shifted to the public. Moreover, the saving of the high transaction costs involved in the detailed checking of standard business terms could also bring competition advantages in the transactions of the contractual partner with end consumers. This would lead to the result that the less the B2B contractual partner checks the standard business terms, the more profits they will make.

The above argument concerning high transaction costs can be justified by some other factors. If the transaction costs cannot be expected to be borne by certain kinds of contractual partners considering their economic strength or ability, there is a justification to exempt them from these transaction costs. The aforementioned kinds of contractual partners include consumers, B2B contractual partners outside the core business and small and micro-enterprises. Importantly, the former two kinds are already subject to relatively strict control. The emphasis here is the small and medium enterprises.

This is because the profit from the business is possible to make up for the transaction cost when the economic strength of the two parties is equal, and the transaction is in the core business field. If the making up of the cost is not achieved, it is a matter of the market mechanism rather than a case for judicial control.

When the economic strength of both parties to the contract is significantly unbalanced, the ability to bear transaction costs is significantly different so that the same transaction costs have totally different meanings for both parties. The most prominent manifestation of this imbalance in the economic strength of

347 Cf. BGH, NJW 1989, 943 (947).

348 Cf. Palandt/Grüneberg vor § 305, Rn. 8.

349 Cf. Wagner, ZEuP 2007, 180 (197).

parties is that a large enterprise may use standard business terms against a small or micro-enterprise.[350] The larger the scale of the business is, the smaller the marginal cost to check or draft standard business terms is. The smaller the scale of the business is, the greater the marginal cost to check or draft standard business terms is. Therefore, the same transaction cost which is not worth mentioning from the perspective of a large enterprise drafting party, may be unbearable from the perspective of a small- or micro-enterprise contractual partner. As a result, the standard business terms used by a large enterprise against small or micro-enterprises are a typical manifestation of market failure caused by transaction costs.

The business size of the contractual partner is connected to but different from the economic inferiority of the contractual partner. At the practical level, there is no doubt that the control of standard business terms in B2B transactions also grants protection to the economic inferior.[351] However, a connection between the use of standard business terms and economic imbalance usually cannot be proved in B2B transactions.[352] Thus, the criteria of economic inferiority will be too rigid to be the only deciding factor as to whether the control of standard business terms applies.

The business size could even play the role of an indicator to prove that the contractual partner is not able to bear high transaction costs to check the standard business terms in detail and makes cost–benefit analysis simpler and more comprehensive. Moreover, only where the contractual partner is too economically inferior to bear the transaction costs of checking the standard business terms in detail, is it justified to protect the contractual partners through judicial control even if they had the chance to check the standard business terms but gave up in order to avoid the transaction costs. Even if a contractual partner within the core business is not able to bear high transaction costs to check the standard business terms in detail, this contractual partner should not be so strongly protected as consumers or B2B contractual partners outside their core business.

2.3 Economic Dependence

Self-determined decision-making by the contractual partner should be the material criteria in the B2B field to differentiate between controllable and non-controllable standard business terms.

---

350 Kemper, S. 31.

351 Leuschner, JZ 2010, 875 (878).

352 Hommelhoff/Wiedemann, ZIP 1993, 562 (566); Hannemann, AnwBl 2012, 314 (314).

To secure the self-determined decision is first to ensure the contractual partner has enough information to defend themself, and this is usually not a problem for the contractual partner in their core business, so long as they are not a small- or micro-enterprise. However, impairment of the self-decision of the contractual partner arises if they are not able to implement their decision based on the available information in the context of the conclusion of the contract. Especially if, despite understanding the disadvantageous effects of the standard business terms, the contractual partner is forced to conclude the contract. In this situation, the standard business terms should be checked by the courts since contractual justice is jeopardized.[353]

Here the transaction costs are not the main concern as the contractual partner did not give up the checking of standard business terms, and the transaction costs are also not proportional to the profit. The contractual partners are not able to refuse them because of economic considerations (economic dependence). The key to the determination of this economic dependence should be that the contractual partner cannot be expected to deny the conclusion of the contract.[354]

An example in the automotive supplier industry is that automobile manufacturers can often dictate the terms of the contract to their suppliers and suppliers are regularly dependent on certain automobile manufacturers.[355] An argument that could be used to justify this phenomenon is that the suppliers could offset those disadvantages to the end consumers. This opinion is not tenable though, because this offsetting would mean a rise in prices and inferiority in competition.

In German literature, it is suggested that laws in other fields could be used as a reference in the determination of economic dependence, such as § 20 I GWB, which is applied to determine the dysfunction of private autonomy and thus could also possibly justify the control of standard business terms.[356] Accordingly, economic dependence can be specified in different forms.

According to § 20 I GWB, enterprises are subject to a prohibition of hindrance and discrimination if they are dependent as suppliers or buyers of a certain type of good or service with no sufficient or reasonable opportunities to switch to another enterprise for such transactions.[357] In other words, there is

353 Cf. Stomps S. 283.
354 Cf. Stomps S. 283.
355 Cf. Stomps, S. 284.
356 Cf. Becker, WM 1999, 709 (716).
357 Cf. Lettl, S. 325 f.

a lack of an alternative and reasonable transaction channel.[358] That makes one enterprise dependent on the other. As a result, the dependent enterprise can be more or less forced to conclude a contract with the enterprise on which it is dependent. This is because a situation without a reasonable alternative for the contractual partner means that there is no freedom for self-determined decision-making for the contract partner even if the standard business terms are easy to understand and their legal consequence is obvious.[359] This form of economic dependence is called enterprise-related dependence.[360] An example of this is where suppliers align their production with the special requirements of motor vehicle manufacturers and make very substantial investments that would largely be devalued if the contractual relationship were suddenly terminated.[361] Another example is long-term supply relationships between an enterprise and its long-term sales representatives, franchisees, or authorized dealers.[362] In these examples, specially made investments by the contractual partner would become worthless, and the existence of the contractual partner could regularly be threatened if they permanently lose the user as the only buyer of their special products and services.[363]

Another form of economic dependence is the shortage-related dependence arising where certain products or services are no longer available in sufficient quantities due to a shortage of supply. This means that customers become dependent on purchasing them from a few suppliers and are unable to obtain these products or services from other suppliers under workable competitions[364] due to labor disputes, a state embargo,[365] or even a pandemic. The unfair terms that the contractual partner faces in this situation could be higher prices or longer delivery time but also unreasonable standard business terms which should be subject to stricter control.

The third form of economic dependence, in the reverse direction, is demand-related dependency. The demand-related dependency occurs when a provider of certain goods or services does not have sufficient and reasonable options to switch to other buyers and is therefore dependent on the supply of the stronger

358 Cf. Emmerich, S. 264 f.; Stomps, S. 286.
359 Stomps, S. 289.
360 Cf. BGH Urt. v. 23.02.1988, Rn. 18 f.
361 Cf. Emmerich, S. 267
362 Cf. Immenga/Mestmäcker/Markert GWB § 20 Rn. 71.
363 Stomps, S. 287.
364 Bunte/Shultz GWB § 20 Rn. 70.
365 MünchKommGWB/K. Westernmann GWB § 20 Rn. 49.

market buyers in order to maintain its competitiveness.[366] The differences of the demand-related dependency from the enterprise-related dependency are that demand-related dependence does not have to be oriented to one sole enterprise in a stronger position and it also could be caused by a high proportion of sales.[367] Assortment-related dependency is understood as a situation in which the supply of certain products of a certain brand or brands could affect the competitiveness of dealers such as wholesalers or retailers. Assortment-related dependency is to be divided into two categories: top position-related dependence and top group-related dependence. The former means the dealer must supply a certain brand of product to its consumers. The latter means the dealer must supply a group of certain brands to its consumers.[368]

The economic dependency from § 20 I GWB has to be further developed independently for the control of standard business terms by the case law and legal studies in order to detach it from its antitrust background and make it suitable for the context of the control.[369] The use of an unreasonably disadvantageous standard business term does not necessarily result in a breach of § 20 I GWB since the standard business term does not have to contravene the purpose of GWB and restrain competition.[370] However, there is an opinion about the connection between GWB and content control, stating that discrimination in the sense of GWB should necessarily lead to an unreasonable disadvantage in the sense of § 307 BGB in order to achieve a congruence of the two legal assessments.[371] The opposite opinion is that a standard business term used by powerful enterprises with anti-competitive effects in breach of GWB, possibly causes no unreasonable disadvantage to the contractual partner within the meaning of § 307 BGB from the objectively and generally viewed.[372] This is because of the difference between the individual weighing of interests in the sense of GWB and the individual, general weighing of interests in the sense of § 307 ff. BGB.[373]

Although the discrimination in GWB may not simply be equivalent to content control, it is undeniable that when contractual partners have economic dependence on users of standard business terms within the meaning of § 20

366 Immenga/Mestmäcker/Markert GWB § 20 Rn. 77.
367 Cf. MünchKommGWB/K. Westernmann § 20 GWB, Rn. 43.
368 Cf. Lange/Bunte/Nothdurft § 20 GWB Rn. 38 ff.
369 Cf. Stomps, S. 288.
370 Wolf/Pfeiffer § 307, Rn. 60; Hoyningen-Huene, Rn. 119.
371 Graf v. Westphalen, NJW1982, 2467; Stoffels, Rn. 411.
372 Ulmer/ Fuchs vor. § 307 Rn. 86.
373 Wolf/Pfeiffer § 307 Rz. 59; Staudinger/Wendland § 307 Rn. 51.

I GWB, the users have a stronger position than those upon whom there is no dependence of contractual partners. The users with this stronger position are able to impose their wills on the contractual partners and impair their self-determination. Therefore, even if discrimination in GWB and content control cannot be simply equated, using the economic dependence in the sense of § 20 I GWB can still help in selecting stricter or looser criteria for the determination of standard business terms or for content control. This will mean that the control of standard business terms is more in line with the protection demands of contract partners and is more suitable to B2B transactions with different degrees of contractual freedom. In other words, the economically dependent contractual partners deserve more protection by means of the criteria of civil law rather than the criteria of GWB.

2.4 A Contractual Value Limit for the Exemption from the Control?

There are proposals that B2B contracts should generally be exempt from content control if they exceed a certain contract value.

A value limit is directly linked to the costs for the contractual partner to check standard business terms and to introduce necessary negotiations (transaction costs). The value limit is thought to be particularly suitable for solving those cases where it is necessary to judge whether the contract is based on a self-determined decision and thus should be exempt from the control of standard business terms. Where a negotiation is deliberately omitted by a contractual partner because of transaction costs above a certain level of the contract value, the contract should be considered a result of private autonomy and be not judicially controllable. In this situation, the contract partner who fails to undertake a negotiation is worthy of little protection.[374] Another argument for this value limit is an increase in legal certainty because both sides usually know the value of the contract.[375] Both sides will therefore also know whether it is subject to the control of standard business terms. Accordingly, they can attribute suitable sources to check the standard business terms and introduce negotiations, if necessary, based on the value of the contract that was being concluded. The approach of using a contractual value limit to exempt the contract as a whole partly or entirely from control of standard business terms, could also be defended by the balance between personal responsibility and legal protection because the contractual partner who has not

374 Miethaner, NJW 2010, 3121 (3127).
375 Becker JZ 2010, 1098 (1104).

taken the reasonable opportunity to negotiate the standard business terms does not deserve to be protected.[376]

The approach of contractual value limit also has problems. The all-or-nothing approach of the contractual value limit does not always seem to be linked directly to "the reasonable opportunity" as a premise of the exemption from the control.[377] Also, finding out the exact value of a contract or contracts of one transaction leads to legal uncertainty.[378] What is more, even if an exact contractual value could be determined by the legislation for the exemption, its meaning for different B2B transactions would be distinct.[379] Its meaning for a certain B2B contractual partner can also change along with inflation and fluctuations in the prices of products or services of the contract. That is to say, it is nearly impossible for legislation to set a general, stable, and proper value limit for all kinds of B2B transactions. More importantly, the basis of this approach, the calculation of transaction cost-contractual value relation[380], also has a deficit. The contractual value is not equal to the profit from the contract although there is a positive correlation between them. And the transaction cost is also to increase with a higher contractual value because of complications of standard business terms.

In fact, there is always a dispute on the exact contractual value.[381] Although it is difficult to deny that the higher the contract value is, the more likely the contractual check and negotiation of the standard business terms are, it is impossible to set an exact number for the exemption from the factual view to draw the boundary between negotiated terms and non-negotiated terms because the number is based on speculation instead of an observation of the factors in the process of the contractual conclusion. Rather, this speculation could indeed be transferred to a decision of legal policy based on a political decision for the economy[382] but is hardly tenable in a factual analysis or a purely legal analysis.

There will be no need to set this value limit generally for all transactions if proper criteria, suitable to the concrete needs for the protection of B2B contractual partners, are introduced. An "all-or-nothing" approach is not necessary, but

376 Cf. Leuschner, AcP 207 (2007), 491 (524).
377 See Chapter 2, part 5.9 of this dissertation.
378 Cf. Huth, S. 315.
379 See Chapter 4, part 2.4 of this dissertation.
380 Leuschner, AcP 207 (2007), 491(524).
381 For example, 1 Mio. Euro of Leuschner JZ 2010, 875 (883 f.); at least 550,000 Euro of Leyens/Schäfer AcP 210 (2010), 771 (793 ff.); 500,000 Euro of Becker JZ 2010, 1098 (1105).
382 See Chapter 4, part 1 of this dissertation.

this contractual value limit can be especially suitable for some special types of transaction where the introduction of a deep negotiation is definitely a responsibility of the contractual partner and the judicial valuation of reasonableness is difficult because of the economic complications of the transactions and the usually existing arbitration terms[383], such as the M&A contracts.[384] These regulations should be put in special legal documents or the case law instead of the general rules of the control of standard business terms. However, the idea behind this value limit can be included in the evaluation of B2B contractual partners' needs for protection so that the contractual partner who has not taken the reasonable opportunity to negotiate the standard business terms does not deserve to be protected. The classification of B2B transactions and corresponding approaches of control are trying to integrate this idea into the control of specific kinds of standard business terms.

3 The Classification of B2B Transactions and Corresponding Approaches of Control

3.1 The Classification of B2B Transactions

In Germany, § 310 I BGB excludes the direct application of §§ 308, 309 BGB to B2B standard business terms. This fact shows that the German legislator believes that B2B contractual partners generally do not have such strong needs for protection as B2C contractual partners and that the intensity of content control should be based on the needs for protection. As the main legal basis for content control of B2B standard business terms, the application of § 307 BGB in the B2B field also has to consider the aim behind the control of standard business terms in its spaces for judicial evaluation- namely, the protection of the contractual partner against the user's unilateral power to draft contracts. The judicial evaluation thus has to comply with the needs for protection of the respective contractual partner in the specific contract. This aim also applies to other regulations on the control of standard business terms, for example, § 305 I BGB where the determination of standard business terms also has to comply with the needs for protection.

In China, the legislator intends to differentiate B2B and B2C standard business terms[385] although very similar regulations in the Chinese Civil Code and Consumer Protection Law make this differentiation impossible.[386] However,

---

383 Cf. Herrmann/ Lasch, DRiZ 2018, 218 (221).

384 Cf. Leuschner, AcP 207 (2007),492 (525).

385 HUANG Wei, p. 956.

386 See Chapter 1, part 4.2.1 of this dissertation.

this does change the fact that Art. 496-497 CCC are intended mainly for B2B standard business terms in the mind of the Chinese legislator. For example, the new addition of the element "unreasonably" in Art. 497, which does not exist in Art. 40 CCL, gives the Chinese courts more space in the B2B field for judicial evaluation, in which one of the factors to consider is the risks involved in transactions. The risks in transactions are certainly different for contractual partners depending on the business involved, their economic positions and so on. That means the needs for protection of contractual partners are also a vital factor influencing the intensity of content control.

Drygala came up with the idea to reduce the protection of the "normal" enterprises compared with the protection of consumers and the other enterprises with no needs of protection. This classification is mainly based on the existence of the economic dependence defined by German GWB (Gesetz gegen Wettbewerbsbeschränkungen).[387]

However, Drygala does not specify the corresponding approaches of control based on his classification. The criterion of the Drygala's classification is not comprehensive enough. In fact, by considering whether standard business terms are within the contractual partner's core business, whether the contractual partner is a small or middle-sized enterprise, and whether the contractual partner is economically dependent on the user, we can distinguish those B2B transactions that are in need of the control of standard business terms from the B2B transactions without such a need.

These factors are based not only on the need for protection and of transaction but also on the purposes of the control of standard business terms. The introduction of the core business takes into account the contractual partner's information and intellectual inferiority.[388] The small and medium-sized enterprise (SME) factor not only involves the contractual partner's economic and intellectual inferiority but also takes into account the relation between transaction costs and profits.[389] The economic dependence considerations involve the imbalance of market positions between the user and the contractual partner leading to the restriction of free self-determined decisions making in the contractual drafting and the contractual conclusion.[390] Based on these elements, B2B transactions can be differentiated further so as to find out whether those B2B transactions are

387 Drygala, JZ 2012, 983 (987).
388 See Chapter 4, part 2.1 of this dissertation.
389 See Chapter 4, part 2.2 of this dissertation.
390 See Chapter 4, part 2.3 of this dissertation.

more similar to B2C transactions in need of judicial control, or more similar to those B2B transactions with enough space for free self-determined decisions. If a B2C transaction is more similar to a B2C transaction in need of judicial control, it should be relatively strictly controlled. Thus, it can be called a B2C-like transaction. Aside from B2C-like transactions, other B2B transactions can be called normal B2B transactions.

The B2C transactions and B2C-like transactions should be both strictly but not equally controlled because the contractual partners in B2C-like transactions are still enterprises or entrepreneurs that are, in principle, less vulnerable than the consumers and should bear a greater responsibility. Also, the control of standard business terms in B2C-like transactions should not be as strict as B2C transactions. The normal B2B transactions should be subject to much looser control than B2C-like or B2C transactions.

Within the frame concerning the differentiation between B2B transactions (B2C-like transactions and B2B transactions), a looser or stricter control criterion in different levels (such as how to determine negotiations, how to presume the unreasonableness of standard business terms, and how to justify the standard business terms), can be discussed under the classification of B2C, B2C-like and B2B transactions from the strictest to the loosest.

3.2 Corresponding Approaches of Control Based on the Classification in Germany and China

3.2.1 Germany

3.2.1.1 Macro and Micro Determinations of Negotiations

One of the disputes over the German case law is that German courts adopt a micro approach to determine the existence of negotiations, according to which a negotiation of any of the pre-formulated contractual terms is not to be considered the negotiation of the whole contract.[391] In contrast to the practice, the use of contracts drafted unilaterally in the B2B field is a regular method to control risks and costs.[392] This practice should be, to a large degree, respected unless there is a reason to negate its justification because of its restriction to the free self-determined decision of the contractual partner. This negation should also be based on the classification of B2C, B2C-like, and normal B2B transactions. That means the micro determination of negotiations should be, in principle, applied

391 See Chapter 1, part 2.3.1.3 of this dissertation.
392 See Chapter 2, part 2.2 of this dissertation.

to B2C transactions as the contractual partners are not able to make a free self-determined decision regularly. An observation of every single contractual term is preferable to judge the existence of a free self-determined decision cautiously for B2C transactions. The criterion for this observation constitutes a remarkable change of the original content, of every pre-formulated term, which is the same as the present judicial practice.

There should also be a difference between B2C transactions and B2C-like transactions in the criterion to determine the existence of free self-determined decisions or negotiations. This difference could be that a contractual term should be considered an individually negotiated term in a B2C-like transaction even if this term has not remarkably changed, as long as the user has given the contractual partner a reasonable chance to make such a remarkable change, but the contractual partner gave up this chance.

As for normal B2B transactions, the criterion should be based on a macro perspective. That means a much more prominent restriction to the concept of standard business terms in normal B2B transactions. The macro criterion here means that any contractual term in a contract should be regarded as an individually negotiated term as long as at least one of the pre-formulated contractual terms in this contract has been remarkably changed under the request of the contractual partner. That is to say, as long as these pre-formulated terms are in a single contract,[393] a meaningful negotiation of any pre-formulated contractual term will lead to the determination that all of the pre-formulated terms in this contract are to be considered as individually negotiated terms. The remarkable change of any pre-formulated contractual term in a contract guarantees the realness of the negotiation of the whole contract. Once the negotiation is done, there is no need to grant any protection to the contractual partner.

3.2.1.2 Indicative Effects of §§ 308, 309 BGB in B2C-Like Transactions

The indicative effect constitutes another angle for the differentiation in content control. The controversy around the indicative effects of §§ 308, 309 BGB could be summarized as such—German courts have made the indicative effects strong in practice and not suitable to the needs of B2B field.[394] On the one hand, the needs for protection of contractual partners are impossibly the same in all B2B transactions. § 310 I BGB includes not only large companies but also SME as B2B contractual partners, and §§ 308, 309 BGB should not be directly applicable to all

393 Cf. Huth, S. 331 f.

394 See Chapter 4, part 3.2.1.2 of this dissertation.

of them without considering the differences between B2B transactions. On the other hand, a B2B standard business term in breach of §§ 308, 309 BGB should not generally be considered valid as the cases in §§ 308, 309 BGB contain indeed regular disadvantages to the contractual partner even in the B2B field.[395]

Regular disadvantages are more likely to be faced by vulnerable B2B contractual partners than the B2B contractual partners with the ability to defend themselves and to base their contractual conclusion on their free decision. In the frame of this dissertation, the vulnerable B2B contractual partners are the contractual partners in B2C-like transactions, and the contractual partners with the ability to defend and to base their conclusion on their free decision are the contractual partners in the normal B2B transactions.

The contractual partners in B2C-like transactions should expect the protection from content control similar to that of consumers. This protection complies with the indicative effect of §§ 308, 309 BGB, which is indeed very similar to the application of §§ 308, 309 BGB for B2C standard business terms. Based on the self-responsibility, the contractual partners in normal B2B transactions should not expect the above protection from the indicative effect.

For example, § 309 7 (a) should not have any indicative effect on a normal B2B standard business term. For a normal B2B standard business term, for example, a standard business term in a contract within the core business of both sides, the contractual partner is expected to foresee the probability of the injury to life, body and health and to has the responsibility to purchase insurance for this injury considering its huge influence to the core business of their core business, from which they receive their income.

Therefore, a balanced evaluation of §§ 308, 309 BGB, based on the above considerations, means recognizing the indicative effect of §§ 308, 309 BGB on B2C-like standard business terms and denying the indicative effect of §§ 308, 309 BGB on normal B2B standard business terms. That means the practice of the BGH should continue to apply to B2C-like standard business terms. As for normal B2B standard business terms, §§ 308, 309 BGB should not include the indicative effect in its content control.

3.2.1.3 From Commercial Customs to Regularly Used Standard Business Terms

§ 310 I 2 BGB requires an appropriate consideration of the applicable commercial customs. The reason for introducing the applicable commercial customs here

395 See Chapter 2, part 3 of this dissertation.

is to require a different level of control for B2B standard business terms from B2C standard business terms, taking into account the special circumstances[396] of offsetting risks hidden behind standard business terms by the B2B contractual partner, and to guarantee the flexibility necessary for B2B transactions.[397] However, the BGH rulings on § 310 I 2 BGB are limited and lack regularity.[398] It is not clear whether the applicable commercial customs here only include commercial customs within the meaning of § 346 HGB or are to be understood further.[399]

There is a case from the BGH which suggests that a regular practice in a certain business sector can also be a commercial custom within the scope of § 310 I 2 BGB.[400] In this case, a regular practice in the business sector is considered and used to justify the exclusion of liability in a repair at a shipyard. However, if we want to include the customary practice in a certain business sector as a commercial custom under § 310 I 2 Hs. 2 BGB, it needs clarifying under what preconditions a practice could be so customary that qualifies as a commercial custom under § 310 I 2 Hs. 2 BGB.

Another ruling of the BGH on processing fees for loan agreements with entrepreneurs, however, in the opposite direction, refers explicitly to the definition of commercial custom within the scope of § 346 HGB.[401] This ruling ignores the difference between them: the commercial customs in § 346 HBG have a normative function while the commercial customs of § 310 I BGB only have to be given reasonable consideration.[402]

In academic literature, it is often argued that the existence of § 346 HGB itself requires § 310 I 2 Hs. 2 BGB to be interpreted with an independent meaning.[403] Correspondingly, § 310 I 2 Hs. 2 BGB is considered a requirement in order to take sufficient account of the peculiarities and needs for flexibility in content control of B2B standard business terms[404] and of customary practice in a certain

396 Cf. BT-Drucks. 7/3200, S. 8.
397 Cf. Protokoll über die Sitzung des Rechtsausschusses des Bundestags am 2.6.1976, 3109 Rechtswesen, A7/6 Prot. 100, S. 35.
398 Cf. Huth S. 240 ff.
399 Leuschner/Leuschner § 310 Rn. 37.
400 BGH X ZR 54/86 = NJW 1988, 1785 (1788).
401 BGH XI ZR 562/15 = NJW 2017, 2986 (2990).
402 Huth, S. 239.
403 BeckOGK/Richters/Friesen § 310 Rn. 59, 62; Staudinger/Piekenbrock § 310 Rn. 31; Wolf/Pfeifer § 310 Abs. 1 Rn. 25.
404 BeckOGK/Richters/Friesen BGB § 310 Rn. 62; Dauner-Lieb/Langen/Kollmann § 310 Rn. 10; Staudinger/Piekenbrock § 310 Rn. 31; Rabe, NJW 1987, 1978 (1983).

business sector.[405] Therefore, the application of § 310 I 2 Hs. 2 BGB should not just be a repetition of § 346 HBG. The deficit of this approach is still a lack of exact criteria to answer the question of what disadvantages of B2B standard business terms are unreasonable.

In the author's frame for the differentiation of control, the role of the commercial custom under § 310 I 2 Hs. 2 BGB is also important. The concrete preconditions are important for the customary practice to be applied in content control. As a matter of fact, regularly used standard business terms, which are commonly understandable facts and ideas in a concrete business sector, can be taken as applicable customary practice to be applied in content control, namely, commercial customs under § 310 I 2 Hs. 2 BGB to guarantee the flexibility of normal B2B transactions.[406] It is possible for regularly used standard business terms to cover the items often involved in content control. Their regularity will also guarantee their competence as criteria in content control. Huth also shares this opinion calling it "usuality of contractual structure as starting point for content control" (Üblichkeit der Vertragsgestaltung als Anknüpfungspunkt für die Inhaltskontrolle).[407] The difference is, Huth does not connect her opinion to the classification of B2B transactions.

A determination of a regularly used standard business term could be similar to that of a commercial custom under § 346 HGB but under lower requirements. It has to be determined whether a standard business term is regular in a certain range of a sector of business or in a geographic area; whether this standard business term is actually used for a long enough time; and whether it is thought to be reasonable by a significant proportion of the participants of similar transactions in this range.[408] If a contractual term is used by a majority in similar business dealings, this is evidence that its use is not only the result of a regularly existing negotiation imbalance but is actually generally accepted as appropriate in the relevant B2B business transactions.[409] This standard business term does not have to be accepted by the participants as a norm, which is only necessary for a commercial custom within the meaning of § 346 HGB.[410]

---

405 MüKoBGB/Basedow § 310. Rn. 17.

406 Cf. Huth, S. 341 f.

407 Huth, S. 341.

408 Huth, S. 342.

409 Huth, S. 342.

410 About the normative force of commercial customs see BGH NJW 1952, 257; WM 1984, 1000 (1002) = BeckRS 1984, 05233; NJW 1994, 659 (660); OLG Köln NJW-RR 1998, 926.

Regularly used standard business terms should be considered, under § 310 I 2 Hs. 2 BGB, a justification for the standard business terms that would be thought unreasonable otherwise, especially in normal B2B transactions under the classification of this chapter. As for B2C transactions, they are certainly not within the scope of regularly used standard business terms because consumers should not be bound by the special commercial practice. The remaining question concerns the role of regularly used standard business terms in B2C-like transactions. The answer to this question will be different when considering different elements. Where the contractual partner is outside of its core business, regularly used standard business terms should not be applied to justify the content of the standard business terms in question because of the sector limitation of the regular standard business terms, which is similar to the restriction of commercial customs with the scope of § 310 I 2 Hs. 2 BGB.[411] Where the contractual partner is a SME or is economically dependent on the user, a regularly used standard business term should be considered as a justification to a standard business term because the contractual partner is a regular participant of its core business and could be expected to be familiar with the regular standard business terms in this sector.

3.2.2 *China*

3.2.2.1 *The Same Approaches to the Differentiation Between B2C, B2C-like and B2B Transactions*

The frame of analysis for the control of standard business terms in B2C, B2C-like, and B2B transactions is both meaningful to the Chinese Civil Code and the German Civil Code. This is because there is no large difference between China and Germany on the needs of protection for contractual partners and the peculiarities of B2B transactions. However, as the relevant legislative regulations of both countries are not the same, the approaches to the control of standard business terms will be in some respects the same, while in other aspects different. The legislative definitions of standard business terms in the Chinese Civil Code and the German Civil Code are nearly same, and thus the above discussions of the German differentiation between B2C, B2C-like, and B2B contracts on the determination of negotiations[412] should be totally same as the Chinese the determination of negotiations.

411 MüKoHGB/Maultzsch HGB § 346 Rn. 28.
412 See Chapter 4, Part 3.2.1.1 of this dissertation.

Yet, when it comes to content control as the wordings of the relevant rules in both countries, they are very different. Art. 497 CCC has a number of problems in understanding and in practice and requires a proper interpretation. The German experience can be taken into account to help make this interpretation. If this interpretation considers Art. 497 similarly to § 307 BGB,[413] the above discussions over differentiation between B2C, B2C-like, and B2B transactions on regularly used standard business terms[414] will be same as the Chinese approach.

3.2.2.2 *Incorporation Control of B2B, B2C-like, and B2B Standard Business Terms*

What should also be discussed is incorporation control under Art. 496 II CCC. It is not a problem in the German Civil Code because § 310 I S. 1 BGB excludes the application of § 305 II BGB to B2C-like transactions and normal B2B transactions while there is no such exclusion in § 496 II CCC.

Both the drawing of attention to and the explanations of standard business terms, from Art. 496 CCC as well as the requirements of an explicit reminder and the opportunity in an acceptable manner from § 305 II BGB, make up for the aforementioned inferiority of the contractual partner by means of information supply and of increasing the contractual partner's awareness of standard business terms as much as possible.

In B2C transactions, the information asymmetry caused by the unilateral drafting of the standard business terms due to consumers' economic and intellectual inferiority, will mean that the transaction experience will be magnified. Therefore, for B2C transactions, strict requirements of incorporation control should be adopted in Chinese judicial practice: the content with a major interest to the contractual partner should be specially marked and the user shall prove that it has fulfilled the obligation of explanation.

Requirements of the explicit reminder and the opportunity in an acceptable manner from § 305 II BGB should also go on being accepted as requirements for B2C standard business terms. This is because it is better to accept them as part of incorporation control rather than as requirements for contractual conclusion. Only in this way is it possible and consistent to free normal B2B standard business terms from the explicit reminder and the opportunity in an acceptable manner requirements.

---

413 See Chapter 5, Part 5 of this dissertation.

414 See Chapter 4, part 3.2.1.3 of this dissertation.

As for the difference between the drawing attention and explanations and the explicit reminder and the opportunity in an acceptable manner, the drawing attention and explanations of Art. 496 CCC are restricted to the content with a major interest to the contractual partner.[415] Although it helps to highlight risks and this urges consumers to examine important standard business terms[416], limited by the vague definition of "major interest," the protection of consumers is not comprehensive. This is because the vague "major interest" brings about the uncertainty of protection. What is more, it does not comply with the protection needs of consumers to limit incorporation control to the "major interest."

In order to meet the protection needs of the consumer, the standard business terms that cannot be identified as content with a major interest to the contractual partner should be subject to incorporation control with an approach similar to that of the explicit reminder and the opportunity in an acceptable manner. It is not only because the explicit reminder and the opportunity in an acceptable manner are usually thought to be part of the contractual conclusion in the legal theory,[417] but also because the explicit reminder and the opportunity in an acceptable manner are able to protect contractual partners from accepting standard business terms without any knowledge of their content.[418] Because of the restriction of the textual meaning of Art. 496 II CCC, it is not possible to extend the requirements of drawing the contractual partner's attention and providing an explanation to the other standard business terms in present legal practice. Although the explicit reminder and the opportunity are not able to provide protection as strong as by drawing the contractual partner's attention and explanation, they are able to provide a basic protection to consumers in the corporation control.

For B2C-like contracts, the Chinese Civil Code also subjects them to incorporation control under Art. 496 II CCC. This is not completely useless for contractual partners in B2C-like transactions. In B2C-like transactions, the contractual partner is inferior to the user, and the application of drawing attention and explanations can also protect the contractual partner to some degree, especially for SMEs and contractual partners outside of their core business. The drawing attention and explanations of Art. 496 CCC can make up for information inferiority to a certain extent. This is also a supplement to the legal protection of

415 See Chapter 1, part 3.2 of this dissertation.
416 See WAN Liming, 2015, p. 413.
417 See Chapter 1, part 3.3 of this dissertation.
418 See Chapter 1, part 3.1 of this dissertation.

the Chinese Civil Code for the contractual partner in a B2C-like transaction before a blacklist or gray list is introduced. In the meantime, because there are still differences in the protection needs of contractual partners between B2C-like contracts and B2C contracts, it is already sufficient for B2C-like transactions to apply the drawing attention and explanations of Art. 496 to the content with a major interest to the contractual partner. It is not necessary to subject B2C-like standard business terms without a major interest to the contractual partner, to the explicit reminder and the opportunity in an acceptable manner requirements. That means B2C-like transactions are also excluded from part of incorporation control.

In normal B2B transactions, neither the drawing attention and explanations requirements, nor the explicit reminder and the opportunity in an acceptable manner requirements, respond to the particularities of B2B transactions. In terms of legal interpretation, the view found in some judicial practice can be adopted for B2B transactions, which is to simplify the drawing attention and explanations requirements of Art. 496 II CCC to the user's notification to the contractual partner.[419] It should be further interpreted from this practice, that both explicit and implied forms of notification will be accepted, thus making B2B standard business terms part of the contract, without special marks or explanations.

4 Summary

The differentiation between the control of standard business terms within B2C and B2B transactions and within the B2B field should be based on economic and political considerations. Considering economic systems and political ideas in different countries, it is impossible to find a totally identical answer for all countries. This is certainly true for Germany and China. However, a frame to classify transactions into different types, with distinct control mechanisms for standard business terms, can be universally helpful for both countries.

Based on the three elements, namely the core business of the contractual partner, the SME identity of the contractual partner, and the economic dependence of the contractual partner on the user, the author has found that those B2B transactions with stricter control of standard business terms are more similar to B2C transactions than to B2B transactions. Therefore, the transactions can be

419 Beijing Third Intermediate Court 2021 jingminzhong 3482 (北京市第三中级人民法院(2021)京03民终3482号民事判决书).

generally classified into three kinds: B2C transactions, B2C-like transactions and normal B2B transactions.

Based on this classification, differentiated approaches should be adopted in the control of standard business terms.

The first issue in this differentiated control approach is the determination of standard business terms, especially the determination of negotiations. In Germany, the macro approach to determine negotiations in normal B2B should be adopted, according to which a B2B pre-formulated contractual term should be an individually negotiated term as long as one of the pre-formulated contractual terms in the same contract has been remarkably changed under the request of the contractual partner. B2C transactions should be subject to a micro determination of negotiations, according to which a remarkable change of the origin content of every pre-formulated term is the criterion to judge if it is a standard business term. B2C-like transactions should be subject to a restricted micro approach, according to which a contractual term should be considered an individually negotiated term in a B2C-like transaction even if this term has not remarkably changed, as long as the user has given the contractual partner a reasonable chance to make such a remarkable change. The aforementioned approaches can also be adopted by Chinese law as there is no large difference between the two countries on this issue.

The second issue in this differentiated control approach, is the indication effects of §§ 308, 309. The practice of the BGH should continue to apply to B2C-like standard business terms. As for normal B2B standard business terms, §§ 308, 309 BGB should not have any indication effect on content control.

The third issue is the role of commercial customs in content control in normal B2B transactions and some B2C-like transactions. Regularly used standard business terms, as commonly understandable facts and ideas in a concrete business sector, can be applied in content control, under § 310 I 2 Hs. 2 BGB to guarantee the flexibility of normal B2B transactions. It is also possible that they cover the items often involved in content control. The determination of a regularly used standard business term could be similar to that of a commercial custom under § 346 HGB but under lower requirements. Chinese law can also adopt this approach in the evaluation of the reasonableness of standard business terms.

The fourth issue concerns Chinese incorporation control in this frame. The present regulation subjects all standard business terms to Chinese incorporation control which should include not only the drawing attention and explanations requirements, but also the explicit reminder and the opportunity requirements. Normal B2B standard business terms should be totally excluded from incorporation control. B2C-like transactions should be only subject to the drawing attention and explanations requirements that are applicable to standard business terms with a major interest to the contractual partner. B2C standard business terms should be subject to the whole Chinese incorporation control.

Chapter 5: An Interpretation of Art. 497 CCC Based on the Experience of § 307 II BGB

To solve the problem of lack of content control criteria in the Chinese Civil Code, we need to construct an interpretation to help the courts to find criteria for content control in Art. 497 CCC.[420] In other words, the interpretation should transform the circumstances of invalid standard business terms enumerated by Art. 497 CCC into the basis of the legal criteria for content control. This transformation should help understand the meanings of liabilities and the main rights that are the core of Art. 497 CCC.

1 Status Quo of Studies on the Interpretation of Art. 497 CCC

Chinese academic literature has presented almost no meaningful interpretation of Art. 497 CCC in order to make the criteria of content control clearer. The relevant studies on content control mostly discussed theoretical grounds of content control[421] and suggestions for the revision of Art. 497 CCC (or former Art. 40 CCL)[422] as well as the academic backgrounds of Art. 497 CCC (or former Art. 40 CCL).[423]

An exception to the above studies is that there is an opinion to interpret Art. 497 CCC in a way that summarizes all the enumerated circumstances for invalidity to be, "unreasonable disadvantages to the contractual partner" and thus makes Art. 497 CCC similar to § 307 I BGB.[424] This interpretation tries to construct a more abstract criterion for content control but at the same time completely disrupts the structure of Art. 497 CCC because this opinion merges those separately enumerated circumstances for invalidity in Art. 497 CCC.

Another shortfall of this interpretation, is its inconsistency with the direction of development of Art. 497 CCC. Compared with Art. 40 CCL, Art. 497 CCC enumerates more circumstances and separates them more particularly.

420 See XIE Gen, FXYJ 2013, p. 118 fn. 51 (参见解亘:《格式条款内容规制的规范体系》，载《法学研究》2013 年第 2 期，第 118 页，注 51).

421 See XIE Gen, FXYJ 2013 no. 2, p. 104.

422 See LIU Chengwei, FXZZ 2019, no. 3, p. 35; HAN Shiyuan, FXZZ 2019, no. 3, p. 27.

423 See GAO Shengping, HNDX 2005, no. 3, p. 75; QI Chunyi, ZWFX 2013, no. 3, p. 653 HE Xuxu, FXJ 2018, no. 6, p. 173； FAN Xuefei, FLKX 2014, no. 6, p. 110.

424 HE Xuxu, SZDX 2020, no. 4, p. 59.

This development shows that, in the view of the legislation, there should be differences between those circumstances for the invalidity in the view of the legislator.[425] The above interpretation abstracting these circumstances in Art. 497 CCC as "unreasonable disadvantages to the contractual partner," on the contrary, blurs the boundaries between them and treats the circumstances without any difference, which runs contrary to the development direction of Chinese Contract Law to the Chinese Civil Code.

According to the aforementioned view of the legislation, Chinese courts should specify which circumstance in Art. 497 CCC forms the legal basis of each individual judicial ruling to invalidate a standard business term. In this sense, the interpretation that abstracts the circumstances enumerated by Art. 497 CCC is not able to provide much help.[426] That also means these circumstances for invalidity should be, to some degree, differentiated rather than totally merged.

2 Judicial Practice of Art. 497 CCC

In order to figure out how to interpret Art. 497 CCC, the author will firstly analyze the relevant judicial practice in China. Chinese judicial cases do not clarify which circumstances for invalidity should be applied. Some of these cases rely directly on the general principle of fairness to declare the invalidity of standard business terms.[427]

Due to the function of Art. 497 CCC and its comparison with §§ 307 ff. BGB,[428] it is not suitable for Chinese courts to directly apply the principle of fairness to justify the invalidation of standard business terms because it would breach the normal sequence of applying legal rules—namely, from concrete rules to abstract principles.[429]

Although Art. 497 CCC (or formerly Art. 40 CCL) is not so concrete as §§ 308, 309 BGB but also much more concrete than § 307 I BGB. Chinese courts should not directly ignore the circumstances for the invalidity of Art. 497 CCC and not apply the principle of fairness directly. Otherwise, the judicial discretionary spaces will be too large.[430]

---

425 Compared with Art. 40 CCL, Art. 497 CCC adds two more circumstances for the invalidity and the element of unreasonableness.

426 See Chapter 5, part 1 and Chapter 3, part 2 of this dissertation.

427 For example Beijing Second Court 2021 jing 01 minzhong 10057 (北京市第二中级人民法院(2021) 京 02 民终 10057 号民事判决书).

428 See Chapter 1, part 4.2.2 of this dissertation.

429 Similarly, in the application of §§ 307 ff. cf. MüKoBGB/Wurmnest § 307 Rn. 25.

430 Cf. Beaucamp/Beaucamp, S. 72; Looschelders/Roth, S. 109.

There are also judicial cases where Chinese courts use the unilateral economic dominant position of the user as their argument to invalidate standard business terms.[431]

The unilateral dominant position often accompanies the disadvantages brought about by standard business terms. However, it is difficult to determine whether the content of standard business terms is significantly disadvantageous to the contractual partner only by relying on the presence or absence of the unilateral dominant position. Even if the user has a dominant position, courts still need to answer the question of why the content of a standard business term in question constitutes an unreasonable disadvantage. In short, the unilateral dominant position is a suitable criterion for checking the content of standard business terms.

Legitimate risks of transactions are also often used by some Chinese courts as an argument in content control.

With regard to the argument of legitimate risks of transactions used by some courts, its role according to the legislator,[432] is one of the elements that should be considered when the courts decide whether the standard business term in question is reasonable or not. Whereas, under Art. 497 CCC, the courts have to find out whether the standard business term has excluded the user's liabilities before this decision of reasonableness is made. Chinese courts need other tools to accomplish this mission.

Therefore, legal principles, a unilateral dominant position, and legitimate risks of the transaction should not be the criteria to compare with the specific content of the standard business term in question in order to judge whether there is, for example, exclusion from the liability of the user or a limitation to the main right of the contractual partner.

A breach of legal rules and inconsistency with the purpose of the contract are also arguments used by the Chinese courts in content control cases and deserve further analysis. Legal rules and the purpose of the contract are generally regarded ways of discovering the liabilities of the user or the main rights of the contractual partner, or, more accurately, tools for finding liabilities.

---

431 See Jiangsu Changzhou Intermediate Court 2020 su 04 minzhong 577 (江苏省常州市中级人民法院(2020)苏 04 民终 577 号民事判决书; Guangdong Foshan Intermediate Court 2018yue06minzhong4014 (广东省佛山市中级人民法院(2018)粤 06 民终 4014 号判决书).

432 See HUANG Wei, p. 956.

The judicial cases where the courts use a breach of legal rules as an argument to invalidate standard business terms do not usually declare whether the relevant legal rules are default rules or mandatory rules. The legal rules in these cases include not only legislative rules, but also administrative rules, and the rules built by judicial interpretations of the Supreme Court of China.[433] However, a differentiation of the involved legal rules in these cases is meaningful. This is because, similar to the interpretation of § 307 II Nr. 1 BGB, legal rules can be divided into default rules and mandatory rules, where mandatory rules play no role in content control of standard business terms.[434] Some Chinese judicial cases have indeed applied default rules in content control although the courts did not mention the differentiation between default rules and mandatory rules explicitly.[435] Based on this differentiation, the default rules are possible to be applied in Chinese content control, which is similar to the German law.[436]

The purpose of the contract is also referred to by the Chinese judicial rulings in content control. In relevant cases concerning the purpose of a contract, the court's attention has been focused on whether the challenged standard business term brings about consequences which would usually not happen with this kind of contract, especially those consequences only beneficial to the user.[437] Therefore, the purpose of the contract plays a role in showing what kinds of consequences a contract should regularly bring.

After the above assessment, it is easy to find that the arguments used by the courts to check the content of standard business terms are not tenable or suitable for content control, except for where legal rules and the purpose of the contract are concerned. Default rules and purpose of contract, which are tools to

433 See Changchun Intermediate Court 2015 changminsizhong 497 (吉林省长春市中级人民法院(2015)长民四终字第487号民事判决书)；Jiangsu Court 2019 (江苏法院2019年度消费者权益保护十大典型案例之三：戴某与环球雅思学校服务合同纠纷案,北大法宝【法宝引证码】：CLI.C.97336730); Shanghai First Intermediate Court 2010 huyizhongminliushangchu 22 (上海市第一中级人民法院（2010）沪一中民六(商)初字第22号判决书).

434 See Jiansu Higher Court 2019 no. 1, p. 29–30(参见江苏法院 2018 年度消费者权益保护十大典型案例之一：从事公共运输的承运人制定的相应 票务规则内容不公平、不合理的，属无效条款，《江苏省高级人民法院公报》2019 年第 1 辑总第 61 辑第 29–30 页).

435 For example Nanjing Gulou Court 2016su0106minchu12385 (例如南京市鼓楼区人民法院(2016)苏 0106 民初 12385 号民事判决书).

436 See Chapter 1, part 4.1.2 of this dissertation.

437 For example Shanghai First Intermediate Court 2016 hu 01 minzhong 6725(例如上海市第一中级人民法院 (2016)沪 01 民 终 6725 号民事判决书)。

analyze the content of § 307 II BGB, are also referred to in Chinese judicial cases. However, the systematic application of these tools, integrated with the wording of Art. 497 CCC, is rarely discussed.

3 The Functions of Default Rules and of the Purpose of the Contract in Chinese Civil Law

We can find that the arguments used by the Chinese courts to control the content of standard business terms, reveal their intention to correct the contracting mechanism. A unilateral dominant position will weaken the legitimacy of private autonomy. The application of legal rules, the principle of fairness, and the purpose of the contract in content control can also be seen to correct the failure of the contracting mechanism. Default rules and the purpose of the contract conform with the above intention of the Chinese courts and are also in line with the positioning of default rules and the purpose of the contract measure in Chinese civil law.

3.1 The Function of Default Rules in Content Control

The function of default rules is to supplement the loopholes of private autonomy. When concluding a contract, the parties often agree on its main points. Afterward, a dispute could arise, and the obligations of both parties need to be supplemented or specified. This requires the courts to create new rules or apply default rules. Among the two options, default rules should have priority because the legislator already balanced the interests when creating default rules. Therefore, the loopholes of the contract should be supplemented by default rules.[438] That means the content of the relevant default rules should apply as part of the contract. Based on this basic positioning of default rules in Chinese civil law, a number of Chinese scholars have advocated for default rules to be the legal paradigm for content control of standard business terms.[439] However, these calls have not been based on the wording of Art. 497 CCC and thus have not constructed a proper legal interpretation.

The role of default rules in content control is connected to the above regular understanding. The application of default rules can correct the imbalance of interests caused by the failure of the contracting mechanism to ensure the justice of the contract where the standard business terms are used. The contractual

438 See ZHU Qingyu, p. 50.

439 GAO Shengping, HNSD p. 73; DU Jinglin, FX 2010, no. 7, p. 29.

partner often only focuses on the essential components of the contract and neglects the content of the standard business terms. However, the information asymmetry brought about by the unilateral drafting of the standard business terms often makes the concluded contract imbalanced.[440] In the case, the law requires exceptional judicial control of the standard business terms that are not usually examined by the contractual partner.[441]

In content control of standard business terms, the default rules should also play a similar role when a contract needs supplements. With the help of default rules, it is possible to amend the imbalance in the content of clauses caused by the lack of contract freedom in the contracting mechanism.

3.2 The Function of the Purpose of the Contract in Content Control

The purpose of the contract is a high-frequency term in the Chinese Civil Code. Art. 511, 563, 580, 587, 610, 633, and 729 CCC all mention the purpose of the contract. The purpose of the contract is mainly used by the Chinese Civil Code to determine whether the performance meets the contractual requirements and to decide whether the contract should be void (because the contractual purpose cannot be achieved). It shows that the purpose of the contract in the Chinese Civil Code is a tool to help judges interpret the contract objectively so that the above determination on contractual performance and contractual cancellation is not limited to a subjective interpretation of contract but adopts an objective analysis of what the contract should be.

This objective analysis is also meaningful for content control of standard business terms. Using the purpose of the contract, the courts can deduce the rights objectively that are indispensable to the contractual partner and also the obligations or liabilities that are indispensable to the user of the terms.[442] The above deduction is necessary in the absence of default rules, to regulate the issues surrounding the standard business term being checked. This deduction is also an approach where the courts create new rules.

---

440 Cf. Huth, S. 25 ff.

441 See XIE Gen, FXYJ 2013, no. 2, p. 113.

442 See Sichuan Higher Court Chinalawinfo CLI.C.64248403 (参见四川省高级人民法院2015年度十大典型案例之五：董小宾与人寿财险青羊公司“盗抢险”保险合同纠纷案，北大法宝【法宝引证码】：CLI.C.64248403).

4 The Lessons from the Civil Law of Taiwan Area

Another perspective from which to observe the connection between default rules and the purpose of contract in the Chinese Civil Code, can be based on a comparison between Art. 497 CCC (applicable in China Mainland) and Art. 247-1 of the Civil Law of Taiwan Area (only applicable in Taiwan and hereafter referred to as TCL), because they are very similar.

The circumstances for the invalidity of standard business terms in Art. 247-1 TCL are "(1) to release or to reduce the liability of the party who prepared the entries of the contract, (2) to increase the liability of the other party, (3) to make the other party waive his right or to restrict the exercise of his right, (4) other matters gravely disadvantageous to the other party."

Art. 247-1 TCL is too abstract to grasp its meaning and to decide which standard business term is invalid accordingly.[443] But we can find that Art. 497 CCC has adopted all of the circumstances for the invalidity of standard business terms from Art. 247-1 TCL. The three points mentioned in Art. 247-1 TCL are quite similar to No. 2 and 3 of Art. 497 CCC. But based on the analysis of judicial practice under Art. 247-1 TCL, Art. 247-1 TCL is too loose to provide any criterion for content control because almost every standard business term would be deemed invalid if content control was strictly based on Art. 247-1 TCL.[444]

There are several similar approaches over the interpretations of Art. 247-1 TCL in the literature. One of these approaches advocates that courts should find the "right" and "liability" of Art. 247-1 TCL in "legal rules", and the so-called "legal rules" here should be same as the "legal rules" under § 307 II Nr. 2 BGB.[445]

Another more concrete approach over the interpretation of Art. 247-1 TCL refers to the standard of the deviations from the default rules and the standard of jeopardizing the purpose of the contract in Art. 12[446] of the Consumer Protection

443 ZHU Baisong, YDFX, no. 54, p. 63, fn. 30; ZENG Pinjie, p. 7.
444 YANG Shuwen, ZDFL, no. 132, pp. 180–190.
445 ZHU Baisong, YDFX, no. 54, p. 63, fn. 30.
446 Art. 12 of TCL stipulates: "Any standard business in violation of the good faith requirements are unconscionable to consumers, shall be rendered null and void. The use of standard business terms is presumed unconscionable where they fall within any of the following: 1. Where the standard business terms of the contracts are in violation of the principle of equality and reciprocity. 2. Where the standard business terms of the contracts, which are excluded by the default rules, are obviously contradicted to legislative intent. 3. Where the purposes of the contracts cannot be achieved due to the major rights or obligations of the contracts are restricted by such terms and conditions."

Act of Taiwan Area (hereafter referred to as CPAT).[447] In this approach, based on the facts that CPAT is legislated later than TCL and Art. 12 CPAT is more detailed than Art. 247-1 TCL,[448] the standard of the deviations from the default rules and the standard of jeopardizing the purpose of the contract should also be applicable under Art. 247-1 TCL, if the relation between Art. 71 TCL[449] and Art. 247-1 TCL is systematically understood.[450]

From the above-mentioned similarity between Art. 247-1 TCL and Art. 497 CCC and the academic opinions over Art. 247-1 TCL, it is not difficult to find that the introduction of the criteria for diagnosing deviations from default rules and of jeopardizing the purpose of the contract is also a possible option for the Chinese Civil Code. The realization of this introduction relies on a more detailed analysis of Art. 497 CCC and a proper method of legal interpretation.

5 The Differentiation Between the Liability and the Main Right in Art. 497 CCC

In Art. 497 CCC, the scopes of the circumstances for invalidity overlap with each other in practice. For example, a standard business term that alleviates the user's liability can also be considered a restriction of the main right of the contractual partner in practice.[451]

What is more serious, is that the exemption of the user's liability and the exclusion of the contractual partner's main right could also overlap. According to the Art. 497 CCC, a standard business term exempting the user from its liability will only be void if the exemption is unreasonable, while a standard business term becomes void when it excludes the contractual partner's main right. The exemption of the user's liability can also be seen as the exclusion of the contractual partner's right. Whereas, according to the Art. 497 CCC, a standard business term exempting the user from the liability will be void only if the exemption is unreasonable while a standard business term excluding the contract partner's

447 See ZENG Pinjie, p. 6.

448 YANG Shuwen, ZDFL, no. 132, p. 201.

449 Article 71 of TCL stipulates: "A juridical act which violates an imperative or prohibitive provision of the act is void except voidance is not implied in the provision."

450 ZHAN Senlin, YDFX 230, p. 34.

451 For example Guangzhou Intermediate Court Chinalawinfo CLI.C.117982588 (例如广州市中级人民法院预付式消费纠纷十大典型案例之五：刘某与某公司教育培训合同纠纷案 ——"课程开课，不予退款"约定无效，北大法宝【法宝引证码】CLI.C.117982588).

main right is directly void. In summary, an exemption of the user from their liability is permitted unless it is prohibited by Art. 506[452] or other mandatory rules. Or, the exemption is thought to be reasonable by the courts under Art. 497 CCC, while the exclusion of the main right of the contractual partner is prohibited by Art. 497 CCC which only prohibits those "unreasonable" exemptions. The overlap between the exemption of the user's liability and the exclusion of the contractual partner's main right creates a contradiction in the test of reasonableness or in the assessment of the importance of the excluded right. If a standard business term could be considered to constitute both an exemption of the user's liability and an exclusion of the contractual partner's main right, it would raise the question whether an additional test of reasonableness is essential.

This is not a problem in § 307 II BGB. Because § 307 BGB has already been concretized by §§ 308 and 309 BGB, § 307 II BGB is only used to deal with those standard business terms that are not regulated by §§ 308 and 309. And although the scopes of Nr. 1 and Nr. 2 also possibly overlap, the sequence and priority of application can solve this problem.[453]

However, there is no such interpretation of Art. 497 CCC. In Chinese law, Art. 497 CCC plays a major role in content control. Eliminating the potential contradiction discussed above, is important for clarifying the applicable rules. Therefore, an interpretation of Art. 497 CCC needs to differentiate the circumstances with the liability of the user as the core and the circumstances with the main rights of the user as the core in No. 2 and 3 of Art. 497 CCC. If the boundary between the scopes of the liability and the main right is clear, there will be no contradiction between the circumstances for the invalidity in Art. 497 CCC.

Eliminating the potential contradiction discussed above, is important for clarifying the applicable rules. Therefore, an interpretation of Art. 497 CCC needs to differentiate the circumstances with the liability of the user as the core and the circumstances with the main rights of the user as the core in no. 2 and 3 of Art. 497 CCC.

452 Article 506: "An exculpatory clause in a contract exempting the liability on the following acts are void: (1) causing physical injury to the other party; or 2) causing losses to the other party's property intentionally or due to gross negligence."

453 See Chapter 1, part 4.1.2.2 of this dissertation.

6 Elements of Interpretation

Legal interpretation requires comprehensive consideration of the semantic element (das sprachlich-grammatikalische Element), the systematic element (das systematische Element), and the historical element (das historische element), as well as the teleological element (das teleologische Element).[454] The meaning of the provisions is often not completely determined by its text.[455] The limitation of the semantic element is that the wording can be multivocal with changes of the context and the literal meaning may also conflict with other norms requiring amendments by interpretation.[456] The semantic element can sometimes at most determine the absolute boundary of interpretation.[457] The system element and the historical element are considered within this boundary.[458]

As the core concepts of Art. 497 CCC are "liability" and "main right", and the circumstances should be differentiated respectively, what is key for the interpretation of Art. 497 CCC, is the clarification of the meaning of "liability" and "main right." Because the function of Art. 497 CCC is similar to § 307 II BGB, the relevant German legal experience should be taken as a reference for the Chinese interpretation.

6.1 The Semantic Element

6.1.1 The Possible Meanings of "Liability"

The core meaning of "liability" in Art. 497 CCC is the first meaning when this word is mentioned.[459] In Chinese legal theory, liability is always described as the legal consequence of the breach of an obligation.[460]

An obligation is the requirement of behaviors stipulated by the law or in a contract. If the obliged person violates this requirement, legal consequences or "liability" occurs. In reality, an obligation and its consequent liabilities are only separated in rare cases.[461]

454 Cf. Rüthers/Fischer/Birk, S. 428 f.
455 Cf. Mike Wienbracke, S. 55.
456 Cf. Rüthers/Fischer/Birk, S. 432.
457 Cf. Wienbracke, S. 55.
458 Cf. Wienbracke, S. 77.
459 Cf. Larenz, S. 354.
460 See SUN/ZHU, p. 162–163； LIANG Huixing, 2017, p. 85.
461 See CHEN Huabin, p. 228.

This is because there will be no consequence for the breach of obligation if the law or the contract stipulates no liability—then the formally obliged person will no longer be factually obliged. Therefore, even if a legal rule or a contractual provision prescribes only one of liability and obligation, it can be inferred that the other is to be prescribed.[462]

Even if the Chinese theory of civil law distinguishes between liability and obligation, a differentiation between them from the perspective of legal effects seems unnecessary. Therefore, "liability" in Art. 497 CCC has both a narrow meaning and a broad meaning. The narrow meaning is the legal consequences of a breach of the user's obligation(s). The broad meaning is the obligation of the user and the legal consequences of a breach of the user's obligation.[463]

6.1.2 *Possible Meanings of "Main Right"*

Clarifying the potential meanings of the "main right" in Art. 497 CCC is simpler than clarifying the meanings of liability. With reference to the cardinal obligation in German case law under § 307 II Nr. 2 BGB and the understanding of Chinese legal theory on the topic of contractual rights and obligations, the contractual partner's right to require the user of main performance obligations is certainly the most important right of the contractual partner and thus constitutes the core semantic meaning of "main right."

In addition to this right to require the main performance obligations, other rights of the contract partner belong to the margin semantic meaning (Randbereich)[464] of the main right. Among them, it remains to be decided, by consideration of the other elements, whether the right of the contractual partner to require the user's ancillary performance obligations and the right of the contractual partner to be protected by the user (the obligations of protection), should also belong to the "main right" according to Art. 497 CCC.

6.2 The Historical Element

When the legislator drafted the Chinese Civil Code, they had clearly distinguished between Art. 497 No. 1 and No. 2, 3 CCC. According to this distinction, No. 1 constitutes the common legal circumstances for the invalidity of all

---

462 See Shandong Qingdao Intermediate Court 2016 lu 02 minzhong 9676 (山东省青岛市中级人民法院 (2016)鲁 02 民终 9676 号民事判决书).

463 See SUN/ZHU, p. 162.

464 About the relationship between the core semantic meaning and the margin semantic meaning in the legal interpretation see Larenz, S. 342.

juridical acts while No. 2 and 3 constitute special circumstances for the invalidity of standard business terms.[465]

Therefore, the legal basis of the liability and main right in Art. 497 CCC, does not include mandatory rules, which are the common legal circumstances for the invalidity of juridical acts. As for the function of No. 2 and 3, the legislator also considered the circumstances of invalidity enumerated in Art. 497 CCC as further concretizations of the principle of fairness.[466] This shows that the legal interpretation should further consider how to clarify this concretization rather than homogenizing all circumstances. The direction of development from the Chinese Contract Law to the Chinese Civil Code also gives the same answer.[467]

6.3 The Systematic Element

Precisely, the legal basis of content control is only Art. 497 No. 2 and No. 3 CCC. Only default rules can be the legal sources of liability or the main right since all mandatory rules are already covered by No. 1. This conclusion is similar to the understanding of the "legal rules" in § 307 II Nr. 1 BGB.

The interpretation of the circumstances for invalidity containing the concept "liability" in Art. 497 No. 2 CCC should also be similar to § 307 II Nr. 2 BGB with considerations of the three propositions demonstrated above. These are: (a) the core semantic meaning of the "main right" is the contractual partner's right to claim the main performance obligation from the user of standard business terms; (b) the basis of the main performance obligation is normally contract provisions rather than default rules; and (c) the circumstances for the invalidity in Art. 497 CCC should be differentiated in terms of the scope of application, according to which is the core concept, the liability or the main right.

The core semantic meaning of the "main right"—namely, the contractual partner's right to claim the main performance obligation from the user of standard business terms, is connected to the contractual purpose. Therefore, it is suitable to introduce the criterion of jeopardizing the contractual purpose into the application of those circumstances that use the concept "main right" as their core concept in Art. 497 CCC.

The next step is to figure out the relation between default rules and those circumstances with the concept "liability" as their core concept in Art. 497 CCC.

---

465 See HUANG Wei, p. 956

466 See HUANG Wei, p. 956.

467 From the Chinese Contract Law to the Chinese Civil Code, the circumstances becomes more detailed and distinct from each other.

The analysis here can be done in two ways: focusing on scopes of application or the roles of standard business terms.

From the perspective of scopes of application, although the liability can have a contractual basis in theory, it is only possible that the source of liability referred to in Art. 497 CCC constitute default rules because of the need to draw the boundary between the two kinds of above-mentioned circumstances in Art. 497 CCC, namely, between the concepts of liability and main right. Otherwise, there would be an overlap between their scopes of application and, as a result, there would be a contradiction between the circumstances as their constituent elements would be different. This would lead to a contradiction between validity and invalidity of the same standard business term.[468]

From the perspective of the roles of standard business terms, one of standard business terms' major roles is to set up a contractual provision making the user less responsible for the other party. A default rule should apply directly if the user has not used this standard business term. The comparison between the standard business term and the default rule is certainly useful for the evaluation of the reasonableness of this standard business term. And the "liability" is the most suitable concept to describe the responsibility of the user that the standard business term is going to impair. The alleviation of the user's liability or the exemption from the user's liability can be seen as a breach of the default rule, on which the liability is based on. This understanding matches the roles of standard business terms.

As a standard business term should not be recognized as an individual agreement, the comparison between standard business terms and the default rule is certainly useful for the evaluation of reasonableness for this standard business term. Liability constitutes the most suitable concept to describe the responsibility of the user that the standard business term tries to impair.

Therefore, the basis of the liability in Art. 497 CCC should be default rules. The unreasonable exemption from liability, the unreasonable alleviation of liability, and the unreasonable increase in the liability of the contractual partner are, therefore, forms of deviations from default rules (the same as § 307 II Nr. 1 BGB). This is because all the legal basis of the liability in Art. 497 CCC are only default rules, and the unreasonable exemption, alleviation, and increase of the liability are understood as the deviations. The determination of a deviation should consider the importance of the breached default rules and the degree to

468 See Chapter 3, part 2.1 of this dissertation

which it is breached. This is similar to the usual understanding of § 307 II Nr. 1 BGB.[469]

The system element could also help to check the meaning of the main right, especially the possibility of including into the scope of the main right, the contractual partner's right to require the ancillary performance obligations of the user and to be protected by the user (the obligations of protection).

The ancillary performance obligations play the role of guaranteeing the achievement of the main performance obligations—the right to which are the core meaning of the main right of the contractual partner in Art. 497 CCC. Therefore, similarly to § 307 II Nr. 2, the right of the contractual partner to require the ancillary performance of the user should also belong to the main right of the contractual partner if the ancillary performance obligations are closely related to the main performance obligations or if they seriously and unilaterally affect the interests of the contractual partner. Without these important ancillary performance obligations, the protection of the main performance obligations will be significantly impaired. What is different is the obligations of protection. Because Art. 506 No. 1 CCC stipulates that a contractual term which exempts liability for the act of causing physical injury to the other party shall be void, it is unnecessary for the Chinese Civil Code to include the obligations of protections of the user into the scope of the main right of the contractual partner.

In summary, the unreasonable exemption, alleviation, and increase of liability in Art. 497 No. 2 CCC, should be interpreted similarly to § 307 II Nr. 1 BGB. It should also act as the criterion for determining deviations from default rules and the unreasonable limitation of the purpose of the contract. Additionally, the exclusion from the purpose of contract should be interpreted similarly to § 307 II Nr. 2 BGB acting as the criterion for the jeopardizing the purpose of the contract assessment.

7 Summary

The present studies on the interpretation of Art. 497 CCC do not provide practical criteria for content control. Judicial practice of Art. 497 CCC, shows that among all grounds in Chinese practice of content control, it is only possible for the default rules and the contractual purpose to be connected to Art. 497 CCC and to be applied as criteria. The function of default rules within content control is to supplement private autonomy. The function of the contractual purpose

---

469 See Chapter 1, part 4.1.2.1 of this dissertation.

in content control is to provide an objective analysis of the contract in order to find out what the contract should be, where there is a lack of default rules. The inspiration from Art. 247-1 TCL, which is very similar to Art. 497 CCC, makes it acceptable to interpret Art. 497 CCC with reference to § 307 II BGB.

The interpretation of Art. 497 CCC should be based on the differentiation between the liability and the main right. The semantic, historical, and system elements should be considered in the interpretation. In this way, the unreasonable exemption, alleviation, and limitation of the user's liability should be interpreted as the deviation from default rules. The unreasonable limitation of the main right and the exclusion of the main right should be interpreted as jeopardizing the purpose of the contract.

Conclusion

The comparison between German law and Chinese law on the control of standard business terms in this dissertation is the basis for both the analysis and the solution of the selected problems. The comparison includes references to regulations that are similar but not totally same in German and Chinese law in order to find their commonly faced problems and to show how the German legal experience can support in the interpretation and application of the Chinese Civil Code.

The wordings of the definitions are almost the same. The only difference between the German Civil Code and the Chinese Civil Code from their wordings, is the "multiple-use" in the German Civil Code and the "reuse" in the Chinese Civil Code.[470] However, this difference does not lead to a factual difference in the determination of standard business terms. At the level of the legal practice, the Chinese judicial differentiation between B2C and B2B standard business terms is different from the German case law. Chinese courts tend to adopt a looser control of B2B standard business terms, although their approach is not consistent and thus brings about legal uncertainty.[471] In contrast, German case law treats B2C and B2B transactions similarly on this issue. The approach of German case law significantly limits the freedom of decisions in the B2B field. The determination of standard business terms should comply with the needs of protection of the contractual partner and the needs of concrete transactions.[472] Neither the German approach nor the Chinese approach is perfect because the needs of protection and the concrete situations within the B2B field have not been explored enough in either approach. There should be differences in terms of the determination of standard business terms—not only between B2C and B2B transactions but also between B2B transactions with contractual partners with different needs of protection.

Although both the German Civil Code and the Chinese Civil Code have rules on incorporation control, their content and scopes of application are different. The core of Chinese incorporation control, is the drawing attention and the explanation requirements under Art. 496 II CCC[473] while the core of German

470 See Chapter 1, part 2.1 of this dissertation.
471 See Chapter 1, part 2.3.2 of this dissertation.
472 See Chapter 2, part 2 of this dissertation.
473 See Chapter 1, part 3.2 this dissertation.

incorporation control, is the explicit reminder and the reasonable opportunity to take note of the content requirements under § 305 II CCC. Under Chinese law, the explicit reminder and the reasonable opportunity to take note of the content is considered to be part of the essential requirements for the contractual conclusion rather than part of incorporation control.[474] The German incorporation control rules apply only to non-B2B transactions, while Chinese incorporation control, according to its wording, applies equivalently to both B2B transactions and to B2C transactions.[475] The object of German incorporation control is all standard business terms, while the object of Chinese incorporation control is only the standard business terms with major interests to the other party (the contractual partner). These differences between Chinese incorporation control and German incorporation control show, that Chinese incorporation control sets up stricter requirements for standard business terms' incorporation into a contract than German incorporation control. This strictness also makes it possible for Chinese incorporation control to replace content control to some degree.

The Chinese regulations on content control are totally different from the German regulations, if we only focus on their wording. Art. 497 CCC lists four kinds of invalid standard business terms with very abstract wordings. In Art. 497 CCC, the core conceptions are "liability" and "main right." But, Art. 497 CCC does not give any instructions about what the liability or the main right are. §§ 307 ff. BGB include both general clauses (§ 307 I, II) and concrete lists of invalid standard business terms (§§ 308, 309 BGB). The common point is that the default rules and the contractual purpose can be found not only in the German law (§ 307 II BGB) but also in Chinese legal practice concerning content control.[476]

The positioning and function of Art. 497 CCC are analogous to § 307 II BGB. At the same time, the Chinese regulation, Art. 497 CCC, brings a lot of difficulties with it regarding understanding, and is not consistent with Chinese legal practice.[477] Art. 497 CCC needs an interpretation connected to the practice, on which the German legal experience on the applications of the default rules and the contractual purpose in content control can provide help. What should not be ignored, is that both Chinese content control and German content control need

---

474 See Chapter 1, part 3.3 of this dissertation.
475 See Chapter 1, part 3.2.1 of this dissertation.
476 See Chapter 1, part 4.2.3 and Chapter 5, part 2 of this dissertation.
477 See Chapter 3, part 2 of this dissertation.

the differentiation between B2C and B2B contracts. That also makes this differentiation the common problem faced by both Chinese law and German law.

Except for § 305c II BGB, there is no counterpart for §§ 305a-306a BGB in the Chinese Civil Code. Among §§ 307 ff. BGB, the requirement of transparency under § 307 III BGB and §§ 308, 309 BGB have no counterpart in the Chinese Civil Code either. Most of the prohibitions in §§ 308, 309 BGB can be references for future Chinese legislative changes, adding more concrete criteria to content control. The exception is § 309 Nr. 7 BGB, because its scope and content are already covered by Art. 506 CCC.[478]

There are connections between incorporation control and content control both in German law and in Chinese law. The connection in German law results firstly from procedural economic reasons in the judicial rulings and secondly from control of surprising terms. The connection in the Chinese law was based on the interpretations of Art. 39 and 40 CCL of the Supreme Court. This connection continues to exist in Chinese judicial practice because of the lack of clear criteria for content control under Art. 497 CCC.[479]

The differentiation between B2B and B2C standard business terms is the problem shared by Germany and China based on the comparison between the German Civil Code and the Chinese Civil Code.

In the German law, the legislation differentiates between content control of B2B and B2C standard business terms under § 310 BGB, but the case law blurs the boundary between B2B and B2C standard business terms by adopting the indicative effects of §§ 308, 309 BGB.[480] A differentiation on the definition between B2B and B2C standard business terms in both the German Civil Code and in the German judicial practice is still lacking.

In the Chinese Civil Code, there is no legislative differentiation, but Chinese courts often treat B2B and B2C transactions differently. This differentiation in practice means that a B2B contractual term is often considered to be an individually negotiated term more easily than a B2C contractual term. The differentiation in practice also shows that a B2B standard business term is often subject to looser incorporation control measures.[481] However, without explanations, there are always exceptions to the above differentiation in judicial practice, meaning this differentiation lacks legal certainty.

---

478 See Chapter 1, part 5.2.3 of this dissertation.
479 See Chapter 1, part 6.2 of the dissertation.
480 See Chapter 2, part 3 of the dissertation.
481 See Chapter 1, part 3.2.3 of the dissertation.

This commonly shared problem has had importance attached to it by German literature which brought about a lot of relevant proposals. But it has not yet been discussed much in Chinese literature. These proposals for differentiation contain indicators, criteria, and exclusions of specific kinds of transactions, including various approaches of differentiating between B2C and B2B transactions.[482]

The most suitable path for differentiating B2C and B2B transactions, in the control of standard business terms, should be based on the needs of protection of specific contractual partners. Thus, before setting up a suitable path for the differentiation, it is preferable to classify B2B transactions into distinct groups based on factors influencing the possibility of the contractual partner's self-determined decision. The core business of the contractual partner decides whether the contractual partner has enough experience and incentive to introduce negotiations.[483] If the contractual partner is an SME, it also deserves more protection against standard business terms because of the disproportion between transaction costs and profits.[484] The economic dependence deprives the contractual partner of the chance to make a self-determined decision and thus justifies a higher degree of protection for the contractual partner.[485] In consideration with the core business of the contractual partner, whether the contractual partner is an SME, and whether the contractual partner has an economic dependence on the user, the B2C, B2C-like, and B2B standard business terms should be subject to different intensities of control.

As for the definition of standard business terms, a macro approach to determining negotiations in normal B2B transactions should be adopted, according to which a B2B pre-formulated contractual term should be considered an individually negotiated term as long as one of the pre-formulated contractual terms in the same contract has been remarkably changed under the request of the contractual partner. B2C transactions should be subject to a micro determination of negotiations, according to which a remarkable change of the original content of a pre-formulated contractual term constitutes the criterion to judge whether it is a standard business term. B2C-like transactions should be subject to a restricted micro approach, according to which a contractual term should be considered an individually negotiated term even if this term has not remarkably changed, as long as the user had given the contractual partner a reasonable chance to

482 See Chapter 2, part 5 of the dissertation.
483 See Chapter 4, part 2.1 of the dissertation.
484 See Chapter 4, part 2.2 of the dissertation.
485 See Chapter 4, part 2.3 of the dissertation.

make such a remarkable change (but the contractual partner did not take this chance).[486] The aforementioned approaches can also be adopted by Chinese law as there is no major difference between the two countries on this issue.

In content control, the practice of the BGH on the indicative effect of §§ 308, 309 BGB should continue to apply to B2C-like standard business terms. As for normal B2B standard business terms, §§ 308, 309 BGB should not have any indicative effect in the content control measures.[487] Regularly used standard business terms as commonly understandable facts and ideas in a concrete business sector can be applied in content control under § 310 I 2 Hs. 2 BGB to guarantee the flexibility of normal B2B transactions. A determination of a regularly used standard business term could be similar to that of a commercial custom under § 346 HGB but under lower requirements.[488] Chinese law can also adopt this approach in the evaluation of the reasonableness of standard business terms.[489]

In incorporation control, Chinese incorporation control should include not only the "drawing attention" and "explanations" requirements but also the "explicit reminder" and the "opportunity" requirements. Normal B2B standard business terms should be totally excluded from incorporation control in Chinese law. B2C-like transactions should only be subject to the "drawing attention" and "explanations" requirements that are applicable only to standard business terms with a major interest to the contractual partner in Chinese law. B2C standard business terms should be subject to the whole incorporation control process in Chinese law, including the "drawing attention," "explanations," "explicit reminder" and "opportunity in an acceptable manner" requirements.[490]

Content control in the German Civil Code is the most important reference in Chinese legal studies on this issue. The German Civil Code has a complete system of rules in §§ 307 ff. BGB while the Chinese Civil Code relies only on Art. 497 CCC for content control. The positioning and function of Art. 497 CCC is similar to § 307 II BGB which contains two sets of criteria for content control: the deviation from default rules and the jeopardizing of the purpose of the contract. Compared with § 307 II BGB, the wording of Art. 497 CCC is too vague to provide criteria for content control.[491] That leads to problems of legal

486 See Chapter 4, part 3.2.1.1 of the dissertation.
487 See Chapter 4, part 3.2.1.2 of the dissertation.
488 See Chapter 4, part 3.2.1.3 of the dissertation.
489 See Chapter 4, part 3.2.1.3 of the dissertation.
490 See Chapter 4, part 3.2.2.2 of the dissertation.
491 See Chapter 3, part 2.1 of the dissertation.

uncertainty in Chinese legal practice.[492] The introduction of the criteria under § 307 II BGB into future revisions of Art. 497 CCC is certainly an option for the Chinese legislator. However, before these future legislative revisions happen, the interpretation of Art. 497 CCC can, at present, also use the criteria under § 307 II BGB as a reference.

The present studies on the interpretation of Art. 497 CCC cannot provide practical criteria for content control. Judicial practice under Art. 497 CCC shows that among all grounds for content control in Chinese practice, it is only possible for the default rules and the contractual purpose to be connected to Art. 497 CCC and to be applied as part of the criteria.[493] The function of default rules in content control is to supplement the private autonomy of both parties to a contract. The function of the contractual purpose in content control is to provide an objective analysis of the contract, in order to find out what the contract should be, where there is a lack of default rules.[494] The lessons from Art. 247-1 TCL (which is very similar to Art. 497 CCC),[495] make it acceptable to interpret Art. 497 CCC with reference to § 307 II BGB.

The interpretation of Art. 497 CCC should be based on the differentiation between the liability and the main right. Their scopes of application should not overlap with each other. The semantic, historical, and system elements should be considered in the interpretation. In this way, the unreasonable exemption, alleviation, and limitation of the user's liability under Art. 497 CCC should be interpreted as a deviation from default rules.[496] The unreasonable limitation of the main right and the exclusion of the main right in Art. 497 CCC should be interpreted as jeopardizing the purpose of the contract.[497]

---

492 See Chapter 3, part 2.2 of the dissertation.
493 See Chapter 5, part 2 of the dissertation.
494 See Chapter 5, part 3 of this dissertation.
495 See Chapter 5, part 4 of this dissertation.
496 See Chapter 5, part 6 and 7 of the dissertation.
497 See Chapter 5, part 6 and 7 of the dissertation.

References

Axer, Constantin: Rechtfertigung und Reichweite der AGB Kontrolle im unternehmerischen Geschäftsverkehr, 2012.

Bamberger, Heinz Georg/ Roth, Herbert: Kommentar zum Bürgerlichen Gesetzbuch, Band 1, 3. Aufl. 2012 (cited as Bamberger/Roth/Bearbeiter BGB).

Bastian, Günther/ Böhm, Klaus R.: Schutz der Kaufleute vor Allgemeinen Geschäftsbedingungen, BB 1974, 110.

Baudenbacher, Carl: Braucht die Schweiz ein AGB-Gesetz?, ZBJV 123 (1987), 505.

Beaucamp, Guy/ Beaucamp, Jakob: Methoden und Technik der Rechtsanwendung, 4 Aufl. 2019.

Becker, Felix: Die Reichweite der AGB-Inhaltskontrolle im unternehmerischen Geschäftsverkehr aus teleologischer Sicht, JZ 2010, 1098.

Becker, M., Vertragsfreiheit, Vertragsgerechtigkeit und Inhaltskontrolle, WM 1999, 709.

Becker, Thomas: Die Auslegung des § 9 Abs. 2 AGB-Gesetz: eine systematische Darstellung der Grundlagen des Rechts der Inhaltskontrolle Allgemeiner Geschäftsbedingungen, Heidelberg, 1986.

Behme, Caspar: Anmerkung zu AG Köln, Urteil vom 19.9.2016—142 C 222/16, NJW 2017, 2052.

Berger, Klaus Peter: Für eine Reform des AGB-Rechts im Unternehmerverkehr NJW 2010, 465.

Berger, Klaus Peter: Abschied von der Privatautonomie im unternehmerischen Geschäftsverkehr?, ZIP 2006, 2149.

Berger, Klaus Peter/ Kleine, Lucas: AGB-Kontrolle im unternehmerischen Geschäftsverkehr, BB 2007, 2137.

Bernuth, Wolf H. von: Die Bindung des AGB Verwenders an unwirksame Klauseln—Grund und Grenzen, BB 1999, 1284.

Bunte, Hermann Josef/ Langen, Eugen: Kartellrecht Kommentar, Band 1, 12. Aufl. 2014 (cited as Bunte/Langen/Bearbeiter).

Chen, Huabin: The General Part of Civil Law, 2011 (陈华彬:《民法总论》, 中国法制出版社 2011 年版) (cited as CHEN Huabin).

Clemenz, Susanne/ Kreft, Burghard/ Krause, Rüdiger: AGB-Arbeitsrecht, Köln, 2. Aufl. 2019 (cited as Bararbeiter in: Clemenz/Kreft/Krause).

Cui, Jianyuan: Several Issues in the Legislation of the Civil Code, Tsinghua University Law Journal (Qinghua Fa Xue), 2014 no. 6, p. 43 (崔建远:《编纂

民法典必须摆正几对关系》,《清华法学》2014 年第 6 期) (cited as CUI Jianyuan, QFX 2014 no. 6).

Dauner-Lieb, Barbara/ Axer, Constantin: Quo vadis AGB-Kontrolle im unternehmerischen Geschäftsverkehr?, ZIP 2010, 309.

Dauner-Lieb, Barbara/ Langen, Werner: Nomos Kommentar Bürgerliches Gesetzbuch, Band 2: Schuldrecht, Baden-Baden, 3. Aufl. 2016 (cited as NK-BGB/Bearbeiter).

Dietlein, Max Josef/ Rebmann, Eberhard: AGB-Aktuell, Erläuterungen zum Gesetz zur Regelung des Rechts der Allgemeinen Geschäftsbedingungen, Köln, 1976 (cited as Dietlein/Rebmann).

Dittmann, Klaus/ Stahl, Henning: Allgemeine Geschäftsbedingungen, Kommentar für den Geschäftsverkehr in Handel, Industrie, Handwerk und Dienstleistungsgewerbe, 1977 (cited as Dittman/Stahl).

Drygala, Tim: Die Reformdebatte zum AGB-Recht im Lichte des Vorschlags für ein einheitliches europäisches Kaufrecht, JZ 2012, 983.

Du, Jinglin: The Paradigm Function of Default Rules in Regulating Standard Business Terms, Legal Science (Fa Xue), 2010 no. 7, p. 29 (杜景林:《合同规范在格式条款规制中的范式作用》, 载《法学》2010年第7期, 第29页以下) (cited as DU Jinglin, FX 2010, no. 7).

Emmerich, Volker/ Lange, Knut Werner: Kartellrecht, München, 14. Aufl. 2018.

Erman, Walter: Kommentar zum Bürgerlichen Gesetzbuch, Band I: §§ 1–758, Köln, 14. Aufl. 2011 (cited as Erman/Bearbeiter BGB).

Fan, Xuefei: Unfair Contract Terms, Science of Law (Fa Lv Ke Xue) 2016 no. 6, p. 110 (范雪飞:《论不公平条款制度——兼论我国显失公平制度之于格式条款》, 载《法律科学》2014 年第 6 期, 第 110 页以下) (cited as FAN Xuefei, FLKX 2014, no. 6).

Flume, Werner: Allgemeiner Teil des Bürgerlichen Gesetzbuch, Zweiter Band: Das Rechtsgeschäft, Berlin, 3. Aufl. 1979.

Fornasie, Matteo: Schwerpunkte des Kartellrechts 2011: Referate des 39. FIW Seminars, Köln, 2012, S. 113 (cited as Fornasier in FIW).

Gao, Shengping: The General Regulation of the Validity of Standard Terms, Journal of Social Science of Hunan Normal University (Hu Nan Shi Fan Da Xue She Hui Ke Xue Xue Bao), 2005, no. 3, p. 73 (高圣平:《试论格式条款效力的概括规制——简评我国合同法第 39 条》载《湖南师范大学社会科学学报》2005 年第 3 期, 第 73 页以下) (cited as Gao Shengping HNSD 2005, no. 3).

Guhling, Hartmut/ Günter, Peter: Gewerberaummiete, München, 2. Aufl. 2019 (cited as Guhling/Günter/Bearbeiter).

Günes, Menderes/ Ackermann, Tobias: Die Indizwirkung der §§ 308 und 309 BGB im unternehmerischen Geschäftsverkehr, ZGS 2010, 400.

Hannemann, Thomas R.: Der Wille des Gesetzgebers, AnwBl 2012, 314.

Han, Shiyuan: The General Provisions of the Civil Code and the Contract Conclusion, Legal Science Magazine (Fa Xue Za Zhi) 2019 no. 3, p. 27 (韩世远:《民法典合同编一般规定与合同订立的立法问题》, 载《法学杂志》2019 年第 3 期, 第 27 页) (cited as HAN Shiyuan FXZZ 2019, no. 3).

Han, Shiyuan: A Study on Terms of Liabilities' Exclusion, Civil and Commercial Law Review, 1994 vol. 2 (韩世远: 《免责条款研究》, 《民商法论丛》第 2 卷, 北京: 法律出版社, 1994 年) (cited as HAN Shiyuan CCLR 1994 vol. 2).

Hau, Wolfgang/ Poseck, Roman: Beck'scher Online Kommentar BGB, 60. Edition (Stand: 01.11.2021), (zitiert: BeckOK-BGB/Bearbeiter).

Heinrich, Christian: Formale Freiheit und materiale Gerechtigkeit, Tübingen, 2000.

Hellwege, Phillip: Allgemeine Geschäftsbedingungen, einseitig gestellte Vertragsbedingungen und die allgemeine Rechtsgeschäftslehre, Tübingen, 2010.

Herrmann, Ulrich/ Lasch, Thomas: AGB-Recht für Unternehmen auf dem Prüfstand, DRiZ 2018, 218.

Hertel, Bernd Ohlendorf von: Kontrolle von Allgemeinen Geschäftsbedingungen im kaufmännischen Geschäftsverkehr gemäß § 24 AGB-Gesetz, Heidelberg, 1988.

He, Xuxu: The Explanation of Content Control Norm in the Civil Code, Journal of Soochow University (Philosophy & Social Science Edition) (Su Zhou Da Xue Xue Bao) 2020 no. 4，p. 55（贺栩栩:《民法典格式条款的效力审查规范解读——以零时生效条款和等待期条款为例》载 《苏州大学学报（哲学社会科学版）》2020 年第 4 期) (cited as HE Xuxu SZDX 2020 no. 4).

He, Xuxu: Commentary on the Latter Part of Art. 40 of Contract Law (the Effects of Standard Terms), Fa Xue Jia 2018, no. 6, p. 173 (贺栩栩: 《合同法第 40 条后段（格式条款效力审查）评注》, 载《法学家》2018 年第 6 期, 第 173 页以下) (cited as HE Xuxu, FXJ 2018, no. 6).

Hillermeier, Karl: Freiheit und soziale Verantwortung im Vertragsrecht, BB 1976, 725.

Hippel, Elike von: Verbraucherschutz, Tübingen, 1974.

Hommelhoff, Peter/ Wiedenmann, Kai-Udo: Allgemeine Geschäftsbedingungen gegenüber Kaufleuten und unausgehandelte Klauseln in Verbraucherverträgen, ZIP 1993, 562.

Hoyningen-Huene, Gerrick von/ Boemke, Burkhard/ Löwe, Walter: Die Inhaltskontrolle nach § 9 AGB-Gesetz , Heidelberg, 1991 (cited as Hoyningen-Huene).

Höfling, Wolfram: Vertragsfreiheit: Eine grundrechtsdogmatische Studie Taschenbuch, Heidelberg, 1991.

Huang, Wei: Interpretation of the Civil Code of the People's Republic of China, 2020 (黄薇主编:《中华人民共和国民法典释义（中）》, 法律出版社 2020 年版) (cited as HUANG Wei).

Huth, Elise: Kontrolle, Allgemeiner Geschäftsbedingungen im unternehmerischen Geschäftsverkehr unter Berücksichtigung geltender Gewohnheiten und Gebräuche, Berlin, 2017.

Immenga, Ulrich/ Mestmäcker, Ernst-Joachim: Wettbewerbsrecht: GWB, München, 5. Aufl. 2014 (cited as Immenga/Mestmäcker/Bearbeiter).

Jansen, Nils: Klauselkontrolle im europäischen Privatrecht: ein Beitrag zur Revision des Verbraucheracquis, ZEuP 2010, 69.

Jauernig, v. Rolf Stürner: Bürgerliches Gesetzbuch, München, 18. Aufl. 2021 (cited as Jauernig/Bearbeiter).

Karatzenis, Fotios: Zur Anwendung der Generalklausel des § 9 AGB-Gesetz im Handelsverkehr, Pfaffenweiler, 1989.

Kemper, Rainer: Verbraucherschutzinstrumente, Baden-Baden, 1994.

Kessel, Christian/ Jüttner, Andreas: Der Vorbehalt der Individualabrede im unternehmerischen Geschäftsverkehr—Zur Abgrenzung von Individualvereinbarung und AGB, BB 2008, 1350.

Kessel, Christian/ Stomps, Andreas: Haftungsklauseln im Geschäftsverkehr zwischen Unternehmen—Plädoyer für eine Änderung der Rechtsprechung, BB 2009, 2666.

Kieninger, Eva-Maria: AGB bei B2B-Verträgen: Rückbesinnung auf die Ziele des AGB-Rechts Konkrete Perspektiven für eine Änderung der AGB-Kontrolle im unternehmerischen Geschäftsverkehr, AnwBl 2012, 301.

Klimke, Dominik: Summierungseffekt von Formular- und Individualvereinbarung zum Urteil des BGH vom 5. April 2006—VIII ZR 163/05—in diesem Heft S. 368, JR 2007, 353.

Koch, Raphael: Das AGB-Recht im unternehmerischen Verkehr: Zu viel des Guten oder Bewegung in die richtige Richtung?, BB 2010, 1810.

Kondring, Jörg: Die „gute unternehmerische Praxis" in einem möglichen künftigen AGB-Recht für den unternehmerischen Verkehr, BB 2013, 73.

Larenz, Karl: Methodenlehre der Rechtswissenschaft, Berlin [u.a.], 6. Aufl. 1991.

Lehmann, Matthias/ Ungerer, Johannes: Differenzierte Unternehmerbegriffe und differenzierte Missbräuchlichkeitsanforderungen innerhalb der B2B-Inhaltskontrolle, in: Standardisierte Verträge—zwischen Privatautonomie und rechtlicher Kontrolle (Kindl, Johann /Viscasillas, Maria Pilar Perales / Vendrell, Tatiana Arroyo Hrsg.), Baden-Baden, 2017.

Lenkaitis, Karlheinz/ Löwisch, Stephan: Zur Inhaltskontrolle von AGB im unternehmerischen Geschäftsverkehr: Ein Plädoyer für eine dogmatische Korrektur , ZIP 2009, 441.

Lettl, Tobias: Kartellrecht, München, 5. Aufl. 2021.

Leuschner, Lars: AGB-Recht im unternehmerischen Rechtsverkehr: Kommentar zu den §§ 305-310 BGB mit Klauselteil, Erläuterungen zur Rechtswahl und Länderberichten, München, 2012.

Ders: AGB-Kontrolle im unternehmerischen Verkehr—Zu den Grundlagen einer Reformdebatte, JZ 2010, 875.

Ders: Forschungsprojekt im Auftrag des Bundesministeriums der Justiz und für Verbraucherschutz—AGB-Recht für Verträge zwischen Unternehmen—unter besonderer Berücksichtigung von Haftungsbeschränkungen, https://www.bmj.de/SharedDocs/Downloads/DE/Fachinformationen/Abschlussbericht-AGB-Forschungsprojekt.pdf;jsessionid=ED434586408701967 08B7785856033A8.1_cid297?__blob=publicationFile&v=4, 2014.

Ders: Gebotenheit und Grenzen der AGB-Kontrolle, AcP 207 (2007), 491.

Ders: Reformvorschläge für die AGB-Kontrolle im unternehmerischen Rechtsverkehr, ZIP 2015, 1045.

Leyens, Patrick C./ Schäfer, Hans-Bernd: Inhaltskontrolle allgemeiner Geschäftsbedingungen. Rechtsökonomische Überlegungen zu einer einheitlichen Konzeption von BGB und DCFR, AcP 210 (2010), 771.

Lischek, Jan/Mahnken, Volker: Vertragsverhandlungen zwischen Unternehmen und AGB - Anmerkungen aus der Sicht der Praxis, ZIP 2007, 158.

Liang, Huixing: Reading Articles and Learning Civil Law, 2014 (梁慧星:《读条义学民法》,人民法院出版社 2014 年版) (cited as LIANG Huixing, 2014).

Liang, Huixing: Generel Theory of the Civil Law, 2017 (梁慧星:《民法总论》,法律出版社 2017 年版) (cited as LIANG Huixing, 2017).

Liu, Chengwei: The Proposal to the Civil Code, Journal of Legal Science (Fa Xue Za Zhi) 2019 no. 3, p. 31 (刘承韪:《民法典合同编的立法建议》, 载《法学杂志》2019 年第 3 期) (cited as LIU Chengwei, FXZH 2019, no. 3).

Lindacher, Richterliche: Inhaltskontrolle Allgemeiner Geschäftsbedingungen und Schutzbedürftigkeit des Kunden, BB 1972, 296.

Looschelders, Dirk: Schuldrecht AT, München, 18. neu bearbeitete Aufl. 2020.

Looschelders, Dirk/ Roth, Wolfgang: Juristische Methodik im Prozess der Rechtsanwendung, Berlin, 1996.

Ma, Ning: The Content Control Norms System of Insurance Standard Terms, Peking University Law Journal (Zhong Wai Fa Xue), 2015, no. 5, p. 1197 (马宁: 保险格式条款内容控制的规范体系, 载《中外法学》2015 年第 5 期, 第 1197 页) (cited as MA Ning, ZWFX 2015, no. 5).

Maier-Reimer, Georg/ Niemeyer, Christoph: Unternehmenskaufvertrag und AGB-Recht, NJW 2015, 1713.

Miethaner, Tobias: AGB oder Individualvereinbarung—die gesetzliche Schlüsselstelle „im Einzelnen ausgehandelt", NJW 2010, 3121.

Müller, Werner: Die AGB-Kontrolle im unternehmerischen Geschäftsverkehr—Standortnachteil für das deutsche Recht, BB 2013, 1355.

Müller, Werner: AGB-Kontrolle auf dem Prüfstand, IWRZ 2018, 153.

Müller, Werner/ Griebeler, Carsten/ Pfeil, Julia: Für eine maßvolle AGB-Kontrolle im unternehmerischen Geschäftsverkehr, BB 2009, 2658.

Münchener Kommentar BGB: Kommentar zum Bürgerlichen Gesetzbuch, 8. Aufl. 2019 (cited as MüKoBGB/Bearbeiter, BGB).

Münchener Kommentar zum Handelsgesetzbuch, München, 5. Aufl. 2021 (cited as MüKoHGB/Bearbeiter).

Münchener Kommentar zum Wettbewerbsrecht: Gesetz gegen Wettbewerbsbeschränkungen (GWB), 3. Aufl. 2020 (cited as MünchKommGWB/Bearbeiter GWB).

Oechsler, Jürgen: Gerechtigkeit im modernen Austauschvertrag, Tübingen, 1997.

Palandt: Kommentar zum Bürgerlichen Gesetzbuch, 80. Aufl. 2021 (cited as Palandt/Bearbeiter).

Peters, Frank: Zur Verjährung wiederaufgelebter Gewährleistungsansprüche, NJW 1982, 562.

Prütting, Hans/ Wegen, Gerhard/ Weinreich, Gerd: Bürgerliches Gesetzbuch Kommentar, 14. Aufl. 2019 (cited as PWW/Bearbeiter).

Qi, Chunyi: German Experience Over Content Control of General Terms and Conditions, Peking Law 2013 no. 3, p. 644 (祁春轶: 《德国一般交易条款内容控制的制度经验及其启示》, 载 《中外法学》 (Zhong Wai Fa Xue) 2013 年第 3 期) (cited as QI Chunyi, ZWFX 2013, no. 3).

Rabe, Dieter: Die Auswirkungen des AGB-Gesetzes auf den kaufmännischen Verkehr NJW 1987, 1978.

Reifner, Udo/ Volkmer, Michael: Neue Formen der Verbraucherrechtsberatung, Frankfurt [u.a.] 1988.

Rüthers, Bernd/ Fischer, Christian/ Birk, Axel: Rechtstheorie mit Juristischer Methodenlehre, München, 6. Aufl. 2011.

Schäfer, Christoph: Anerkannt, gut und bewährt—eine Analyse des Kampfs um das „Klein gedruckte", BB 2012, 1231.

Schäfer, Hans-Bernd/ Ott, Claus: Der ökonomischen Analyse des Zivilrechts, Berlin, 6. überarbeitete Aufl. 2021.

Schlosser, Peter/ Coester-Waltjen, Dagmar/ Graba, Hans-Ulrich: Kommentar zum Gesetz zur Regelung des Rechts der Allgemeinen Geschäftsbedingungen, Bielefeld, 1977 (cited as Bearbeiter in: Peter/Coester-Waltjen/Graba, AGBG).

Schlösser, Tim: Die formularvertragliche Regelung der Durchführung von Schönheitsreparaturen aus rechtsökonomischer Perspektive, Jura 2008, 81.

Staudinger: Kommentar zum Bürgerlichen Gesetzbuch, Berlin, Neubearbeitung 2019 (cited as Staudinger/Bearbeiter).

Stoffels, Markus: AGB-Recht 3., neubearbeitete Aufl., München, 2015.

Stoll, Hans: Internationalprivatrechtliche Probleme bei Verwendung Allgemeiner Geschäftsbedingungen. Ein Diskussionsbeitrag, in: Otto, Sandrock v. (hrsg.), Festschrift für Günther Beitzke: zum 70. Geburtstag am 26. April 1979, 759 (cited as Stoll, in: FS Beitzke 1979).

Stomps, Andreas: Methodik der Klauselkontrolle im unternehmerischen Geschäftsverkehr, Baden-Baden, 2011.

Su, Haopeng: A Study on Standard Business Terms, 2004 (苏号朋:《格式合同条研究》中国人民大学出版社2004年版) (cited as SU Haopeng).

Sun, Guohua/ Zhu, Jingwen: Legal Philosophy (孙国华、朱景文主编:《法理学》, 法律出版社 2015 年版) (cited as SUN/ZHU).

Ulmer, Peter/ Brandner, Erich/ Hensen, Horst-Diether: AGB-Recht, Kommentar zu den §§ 305—310 BGB und zum UKlaG, 12. Aufl. 2016 (cited as UBH/ Bearbeiter).

Uusitalo, Jutta Jasmin: Einbeziehung von AGB im unternehmerischen Geschäftsverkehr zwischen Deutschland und Finnland, Frankfurt am Main, 2012.

Wagner, Gerhard: Die soziale Frage und der Gemeinsame Referenzrahmen, ZEuP 2007, 180.

Wang, Liming: A Study on Several Problems of Standard Contracts, Studies in Law and Business (Fa Shang Yan Jiu) 1994 no. 3 (王利明:《标准合同的若干问题》,《法商研究》1994 年第 3 期) (cited as WANG Liming, FSYJ 1994, no. 3).

Wang, Liming: The Comments on the Control of Standard Business Terms in the Contract Law, Tribune of Political Science and Law (Zheng Fa Lun Tan)

1999, no. 6 (王利明:《对〈合同法〉格式条款规定的评析》,《政法论坛》1999 年第 6 期) (cited as WANG Liming, ZFLT 1999, no. 6).

Wang, Liming: The Study of Contract Law, 2015 (王利明:《合同法研究》(第一卷) (第三版), 中国人民大学出版社 2015 年版) (cited as WANG Liming, 2015).

Westphalen, Friedrich Graf v.: AGB-Recht im Jahr 2003, NJW 2004, 1993.

Ders: Wider einen Reformbedarf beim AGB-Recht im Unternehmerverkehr, NJW 2009, 2977.

Ders: Wider die angebliche Unattraktivität des AGB-Rechts, BB 2010, 195.

Ders: Stellen vs. Aushandeln von AGB im unternehmerischen Geschäftsverkehr—der BGH weist die Lösung, ZIP 2010, 1110.

Ders: Das Dispositionsrecht des Prinzipals im Vertragshändlervertrag, NJW 1982, 2465.

Ders: AGB-Recht im zweiten Halbjahr 2019, NJW 2020, 280.

Wienbracke, Mike: Juristische Methodenlehre, Heidelberg, 2013.

Wolf, Manfred/ Lindacher, Walter F./ Pfeiffer, Thomas: AGB-Recht Kommentar, 6. Aufl. 2013, (zitiert als Wolf/Bearbeiter).

Xie, Gen: The Normative System of Content Control of Standard Business Terms, Chinese Journal of Law (Fa Xue Yan Jiu) 2013 no. 2, p. 102 (解亘:《格式条款内容规制的规范体系》, 载《法学研究》2013 年第 2 期) (cited as XIE Gen, FXYJ 2013, no. 2).

Yang, Shuwen: The Control of Standard Business Terms and the Contractual Freedom, The Law Review of Chengchi University No. 132, p. 163 (杨淑文:《定型化契约之管制与契约自由》,载《政大法律评论》 (Zheng Da Fa Lv Ping Lun) 第 132 期 (cited as YANG Shuwen, ZDFL, no. 132).

Zeng, Pinjie: The Application of the Control of Standard Business Terms in the Consumer Protection Law to Non-consumer Contracts in: Standard Business Terms II on Non-consumer Contracts and Typical Judicial Cases, p. 3, 2019 (曾品杰: 《论消费者保护法上定型化契约规定对于非消费关系之适用》, 载《定型化契约专题(二)——非消费性关系与个案类型》, 元照出版公司 2019 年版) (cited as ZENG Pinjie).

Zhan, Senlin: Social Changes in Taiwan and the Development of Contract Law, Taiwan Jounrnal of Law no. 230, p. 43 (詹森林:《台湾社会变迁与契约法发展》, 载《月旦法学杂志》 (Yue Dan Fa Xue Za Zhi) 第 230 期) (cited as ZHAN Senlin, YDFX, no. 230).

Zhang, Liang: The Study on the Legislation of the Contract of the Chinese Civil Code, The Journal of Sichuang University (Social Science) (Shi Chuan Da Xue Xue Bao) (张良:《我国民法典合同法编格式条款立法研究》, 载《

四川大学学报（哲学社会科学版）》 (Si Chuan Da Xue Xue Bao) 2019 年第 1 期) (cited as ZHANG Liang, SCDX 2019, no. 1).

Zhu, Baisong: The Application and Interpretation of the Civil Law Norms on the Standard Business Terms, Taiwan Law Review no. 54, p. 52 (朱柏松: 《民法定型化契约规范之适用与解释》载《月旦法学杂志》 (Yue Dan Fa Xue Za Zhi) 第 54 期) (cited as ZHU Baisong, YDFX, no. 54).

Zhu, Qingyu: The General Part of Civil Law, 2016 (朱庆育: 《民法总论》, 北京大学出版社2016年版) (cited as ZHU Qingyu).

Zweiger, Konrad/ Kötz, Hein: Einfürhrung in die Rechtsvergleichung, Tübingen, 1984.

Index

www.ingramcontent.com/pod-product-compliance
Ingram Content Group UK Ltd.
Pitfield, Milton Keynes, MK11 3LW, UK
UKHW021014120926
8556IPUK00040B/1142